Sarah Brown's
Best of Vegetaria

From Truro to Inverness, from Southwold to Dolgellau, Britain's most famous vegetarian cook recommends places to enjoy meat-free food.

Sarah Brown's Best of Vegetarian Britain

Includes over 200 restaurants countrywide

Sarah Brown

THORSONS PUBLISHING GROUP

First published in 1989

© SARAH BROWN 1989

British Library Cataloguing in Publication Data

Brown, Sarah
  Sarah Brown's best of vegetarian Britain.
  1. Great Britain. Vegetarian restaurants,-
  Directories
  I. Title
  647′.9541

  ISBN 0-7225-1860-9

Note
While every effort has been made to ensure the accuracy of this information at the time of going to press, you are advised to ring and check details before going to any of the places listed, in case circumstances have changed in any way.

Text illustrations by Juanita Puddifoot.

Published by Thorsons Publishers Limited,
Wellingborough, Northamptonshire NN8 2RQ, England

Typeset by MJL Limited, Hitchin, Hertfordshire
Printed in Great Britain.

10 9 8 7 6 5 4 3 2 1

Contents

Acknowledgements

Trying to cover the whole country without a network of extremely energetic 'spies' would have been impossible. I would like to thank them all — for the amount of travelling they had to do, for taking the bad along with the good and for not giving the game away whilst extracting a wealth of important information. I hope that they managed to *enjoy* their food as well as being critical diners. My thanks to Hilary Bloor and Phil Jones, Marty Cruickshank, Valerie Greenberg, Pamela Knutson, Wendy Lightfoot, Dorothy Marsh, Roselyne Masselin, Beverley Muir, Rita Owen, Ron and Penny Pilcher, Jenny and Graham Pierce, Sue Pready, Jane Robson, Miriam and David Rosen, Christine Smith and Rob Parfitt, Sheila and Brian Street, Marian Usher, Richard Walters, Patrick Wise, Jo Wright and Ged Young, and many other people who set me on the track of somewhere worthwhile.

Also thanks to my mother and sister Deborah for their company and comments on several jaunts.

I am very grateful to Fay Franklin for helping me plan the guide, to Annie Smith and Michelle Clark for seeing it through to publication, and to Harriet Cruickshank for being her usual inspirational self.

All the eating out that I have done has of course been more fun thanks to my friend Paul. He never seems to mind the curious way in which my route choices round the country invariably bring us to places with interesting restaurants!

General introduction

Following on the great success of *Vegetarian London*, I felt it was time to cover the whole of Britain. Interest in and demand for vegetarian food has increased tremendously in the last few years and now there are many more places offering good alternatives to meat and fish.

I spend much of my time travelling around the country and I wanted to share my discoveries with everyone, vegetarian or no, who is looking for tasty, good value food whilst visiting different parts of Britian, be it for pleasure or business.

As with *Vegetarian London*, this guide isn't limited to reviewing wholly vegetarian places, but includes restaurants, pubs and hotels that have some choice for vegetarians permanently on the menu and some understanding of vegetarian needs. I have included as wide a variety of establishments as possible, from tiny cafés and tea shops to grand hotels and top class restaurants. Many of the places included in this book are ideal for parties who want menus that offer both vegetarian and meat dishes.

I have tried to review restaurants where there is some imagination on the menu and not just a token quiche or vegetable lasagne. I've also included many places worth visiting for the surrounding countryside as much as the food, and several craft centres and galleries are also reviewed. What I have *not* included are restaurants that *will* do vegetarian food but only by arrangement. Nor have I listed commonsense places to find vegetarian food, such as curry houses or pizza places, unless there is some extra special reason that makes them worthy of a mention.

I found the difference in the various areas around the country quite amazing. It makes little difference whether the region is particularly popular with tourists wanting to eat out or full of students looking for cheap eats. It seems more a matter of whether enterprising individuals decide to set up shop, or local hotels have the good fortune to have forward-looking chefs or managers. The more imaginative vegetarian restaurants are still often run by devoted amateurs, though professional chefs are gradually realizing that there is a great deal more to our cuisine than just the dreaded omelette and cliché nut cutlet. I hope that guides of this sort will help places to become established and to encourage a wider range of vegetarian food to be offered regularly at more restaurants.

Apart from benefiting from the wider availability of vegetarian food, I noticed some other encouraging trends. Many places I visited were making a conscious effort to use organic produce — fruit, vegetables and flour particularly — as well as wine and beer. The majority of restaurants had no smoking sections, or banned smoking completely, though sadly this is not true in pubs. Many places offered a good range of food suitable for vegans.

This guide is a personal view of vegetarian Britain, with some help from friends, fellow vegetarians and the orienteering fraternity. The places in the book were visited at least once by me or my research team and the reviews are written on that basis. I hope with this guide you will have some good eating out. Do remember that places can change, so, where possible, phone first. Many places are yet to be discovered and I'd be delighted to receive any reports. Bon appetit!

S.E.B.

How to use the guide

The places reviewed are grouped into 11 areas that are covered by a regional tourist board, such as the North West or East Anglia, plus Wales, Scotland and a separate section concentrating on London. Within each area, the towns are listed alphabetically to make it easy for you to find a place. In the back of the book, there are indexes listing all the towns and all the restaurants alphabetically.

The symbols

✓ This symbol indicates that the restaurant, café or pub is completely vegetarian. In most cases the cheese, if it used, will be vegetarian and the eggs free-range.

£ The average price of a three-course meal, excluding wine and coffee.

♿ This symbol indicates those places where it is possible to get to both the restaurant and toilet facilities with minimum or no assistance. In many places it was possible only to gain access to the restaurant, and, in several places, owners said that they were only too willing to help with wheelchairs as the number of steps was limited. It is best to ring and check on this.

🍷 Licensed. Places that aren't licensed may allow you to bring your own. I mention whether or not this is possible in the reviews, but check if you are unsure. There may be corkage charge.

American Express		Café	
Access		Pub	
Diners Club		Hotel	
Visa		Wine bar	
Self-service or counter service		Coffee shop or tearoom	
Table service		Bookshop	
Smoking		Health food or wholefood shop	
Non-smoking		Take-away	
Restaurant		Theatre bar	

9

A note on the reviews

The venues reviewed in the guide have been visited at least once by me or by one of my researchers or recommended by my team of helpers and fellow vegetarians around the country.

The main criterion for their inclusion in the guide was that there should be a choice for vegetarians permanently on the menu so that you could simply walk in and get a meal. We also looked for tasty food, imaginative and well prepared meals, use of wholefoods and, above all, whether it was a pleasant place to eat.

Although we have been searching for the best there is all over the country, there are, inevitably, some areas where it is extremely hard to get anything vegetarian or even wholefood. Of course not everywhere can be outstanding, but I have aimed to make it clear in the reviews what the style of the place is, its good and bad points, and whether it is worth going out of your way for or simply a handy pit stop.

You will see, too, that a tremendous variety of places are reviewed, ranging from very cheap co-operative-styles cafés run on a shoe-string, but completely committed to vegetarian eating, to high-class restaurants that have found it necessary to cater for the growing demand for vegetarian food, but where the standard of the meals may depend a great deal on the imagination of the chef or management. I think it is impossible to make fair comparisons between these types of places, so I have not given an overall rating system. I have instead picked out my own favourite in each region.

Your comments

I hope you have the same enjoyable experiences we have had. Remember, however, that, although the details in this guide were correct at the time of going to press, restaurants are prone to change and so it is always best to check the opening times and choice of menu, to avoid disappointment. I would be delighted to hear your comments about the places reviewed here and any recommendations for places that you think should be included in subsequent editions.

Please use the form at the back of the book. With your help this guide can lead to even greater choice for vegetarians throughout Britain.

London

London is still one of the best places in Britain to sample vegetarian food and I've selected 26 of the best to give you a flavour of what is available. The food scene in the capital changes constantly but as far as vegetarians are concerned seems to improve with more and more choice. New places spring up that have none of the worthiness associated with the word vegetarian. They are smart, sophisticated and above all have developed menus that would win over the most hard-hearted carnivore. Many are run on a very professional basis and this means you can eat out safely in some style. Finding day-time food is now fairly easy, whereas sophisticated night-time eating is somewhat more limited.

Welcomed trends such as no smoking sections and more use of organic vegetables are just as evident in London as in the rest of the country.

Most of the restaurants reviewed here are also included in the guide *Vegetarian London* where over 100 places are listed. Apart from all these, there are in the capital a wide range of ethnic restaurants that cater well for vegetarians.

Do remember that places in London are particularly vulnerable to change and it is always worth ringing up to check details of opening times and so on.

Bambaya

1 Park Road, Crouch End, London, N8
☎ 01-348 5609
🏠 £9

A warm and welcoming restraurant with a spacious feeling and
lots of interesting pictures, plenty of plants and one wall still
decorated with beautiful old tiles with fruit motifs which are
echoed on the menu.

This is a fish and vegetarian restaurant, Caribbean in style,
and there was a wide range of interesting dishes for vegetarians:
such as Hoppin' John, a colourful mixture with ackee (a most
unusual, custard-like vegetable) served with rice and beans; or
Vegetable Rundown, which was a mixture of carrots and
courgettes cooked in coconut milk. There was also a bulgar
pilaff and a more standard curry. For starters you could have a
spicy green pea fritter, but check on the stock used if you go for
the soup. Many of the typical Caribbean vegetable can be had
as side dishes, such as plantain, yams or green bananas, and
there is also cornbread and a terrific arame coleslaw. For
pudding there are delicious heavy cakes and pumpkin pie.

I thought the food was very tasty. Perhaps, for anyone new to
the cuisine, the menu could give a little more guidance on what
goes best together. It might encourage a more adventurous
choice.

Bambaya is busy and friendly, and is an excellent place for an
evening out. They don't use cheese.

Open: 12-2.30, 6.30-11 Monday-Saturday, Sunday 10.30,
       closed Sunday lunch and all day Monday
14, 4, W7 bus to Crouch End Clock Tower
46 seats

Café Pacifico

5 Langley Street, London WC2
 01-379 7728
£8

This is where streetwise latent Mexican bandits hang out when shopping in Covent Garden. You can act out one of those John Huston movies here, what with the ceiling fans, fading yellow walls and long bar. The service is positively American in its friendliness — it is owned by a consortium of Californians — and the food is a good example of its kind. Some of it is even wholefood, using brown flour and so forth. The guacamole, nachos, enchiladas and beans are great, but be warned, you can come away feeling rather bloated with all those beans. Above all, this place is fun and very different.

Open: 11.30-11.45 Monday-Saturday, 12-10.45 Sunday
Covent Garden tube
125 seats

The Cherry Orchard

241 Globe Road, London E2
 01-980 6678
£4

This is still one of the cheapest vegetarian restaurants in
London, and seems to go from strength to strength with an
expanded and more imaginative menu. The atmosphere is light,
relaxed and warm. In the summer you can eat outside in their
little garden.
   The food is simple, reliable and very tasty; good salads, nut
roasts, pizzas and an excellent range of herb teas and fruit
juices. The range of vegan food is good. The cheese is
vegetarian and the eggs free-range.
   At lunch-time it is self-service and during the afternoon, only
cakes and drinks are available. In the evening it changes to table
service, and this certainly creates a more stylish atmosphere.
The staff are very attentive. This restaurant, owned and run by a
Buddhist community, is well worth a visit.

Open: 12-10.30 Tuesday-Saturday
Bethnal Green tube
55 seats

Chutney's

124 Drummond Street, London NW1
☎ 01-388 0604
🍴 £7

A relatively new Indian vegetarian restaurant. The surroundings
are stylish, with a black and white theme.

Service was attentive and friendly, the prices are extremely
reasonable and, above all, the food is good.

I had a main course of lentil uppertham (described in a rather
off-putting fashion as a lentil pizza). It is delicious, lightly
spiced with a coconut flavour. The vegetable curry was good
and the side dish of okra excellent. The special thali is
tremendous, both for its variety and value.

To follow there are the classic puddings of shrikand and kulfi.

I think it's certainly worth going to Chutney's with a good
appetite so that you can manage a main course and some side
dishes, as they are generally splendid and well cooked. At
lunch-time there is a help-yourself buffet for a set price of £3.75.
Again, excellent value.

Open: 12-2.45, 6-11.30 daily
Euston/Euston Square tube
75 seats

Country Life

1 Heddon Street, London W1
☎ 01-434 2922
🏠 £4

A haven for vegan and vegetarian gluttons and surely what must be the best value for money in London. All you can eat for around £4, and all the food is wholesome, tasty and dairy-free though you wouldn't notice.

It is a help-yourself buffet system, priced according to what you eat. Stick with soup, salads, bread and spreads and that will cost you £3.10, add a 'Hot special' and it's £3.50, or go for the lot at £3.99. You get a small tray and appropriate plates then work your way round. I had a delicious Russian potato soup with rye bread and sunflower spread, followed by a heaped plate of different raw vegetables and some tofu and cashew nut dressings. Three 'Hot specials' were available, including a spinach quiche and chick pea stew.

For pudding, there are separately-priced cakes, or a fruit salad in the all-in-one price that can be enhanced with different toppings, such as granola, dried fruits, nuts and seeds.

As you stagger off with your loaded tray, the person handing you your bill (which you pay on the way out) kindly explains that you can come back to the table for as much as you want again, all you do is show the ticket! Drinks are priced separately.

The atmosphere is quite relaxed considering what a busy place it is. You'll almost certainly have to share a table, but it is worth it for excellent food offered in a genuinely generous and warm-hearted way.

Open: 11.30-2.30 Monday-Thursday, 11.30-2 Friday
Credit cards: none
Piccadilly Circus tube
80 seats
🍽

Cranks

(Addresses and details listed on the following page.)

Cranks has, for the last twenty years, been one of the mainstays of vegetarian eating in London. Whilst the flagship still remains Marshall Street, a number of other branches have opened in the last couple of years. Plans are underway to centralize the cooking and baking in one unit that will supply all the branches, thus maintaining even standards but hopefully not formularizing the food so it loses its character.

Food at Cranks has never been cheap, but they don't cut corners in terms of the quality of ingredients they use, nor do they run out of food. The queues are usually long but it is worth waiting to sample the wonderful savouries, salads, puddings and cakes.

The decor is simple, often with bench seating. At both the Tottenham Road and Adelaide Street branches, good use is made of plain wood and lighting, which is very pleasing. There's a feeling that no expense is spared in the design, down to eating off beautiful craft pottery that inevitably increases the prices.

The wine and dine is at Marshall Street. Started some years ago in a small area, it has now expanded and become more sophisticated with candles on the tables and other trimmings, so it is an excellent place for a special night out.

Cranks is professionally organized. It comes in for a fair share of knocks because it is well-established and expectations are higher. Although the food remains the same, it is always well-presented and wholesome. My favourite branches are Marshall Street and Adelaide Street as they are spacious, whereas some of the new places are rather pokey, especially Covent Garden.

8-10 Adelaide Street, London WC1
☎ 01-379 5919
🏠 £5.50 buffet
Open: 8-7 Monday-Friday, 10-6 Saturday, closed Sunday
Credit cards: none
Charing Cross tube
60 seats

23 Barrett Street, London W1 ✓
☎ 01-495 1340
🏠 £5
Open: 8-8 Monday-Saturday, closed Sunday
Credit cards: none
Bond Street tube
35 seats

11 The Market, Covent Garden, London WC2 ✓
☎ 01-379 6508
🏠 £5
Open: 10-8 Monday-Friday, 10-5 Saturday and Sunday
Credit cards: none
Covent Garden tube
30 seats

17-18 Great Newport Street, London W1 ✓
☎ 01-836 5226
🏠 £5
Open: 8-8.30 Monday-Friday, 10-8.30 Saturday, closed Sunday
Credit cards: none
Leicester Square tube
40 seats

8 Marshall Street, London W1 ✓   buffet
☎ 01-437 9431   wine and dine
🏠 £5 buffet, £11 wine and dine
Open buffet: 8-7 Monday-Friday, 9-7 Saturday
        wine and dine: 6.30-11 Monday-Saturday
Oxford Circus tube
170 seats

9-11 Tottenham Street, London W1 ✓
☎ 01-631 3912
🏠 £5
Open: 8am-9pm Monday-Friday, 9-9 Saturday, closed Sunday
Credit cards: none
Goodge Street tube
60 seats

Food For Thought

31 Neal Street, London WC2
☎ 01-836 0239
🏠 £4

Always busy at feeding times, when you will certainly have to
queue down the stairs. The wait can be at least 10 minutes but
it is thought worthwhile, mainly because the food is very
reasonably priced. Main courses are around £1.50 and a mega-
salad is £2.20
   The menu changes frequently and it is all wholesome fare —
tasty savouries and luscious cakes and puddings, and some
choice for vegans. Now real addicts can buy the cookbook
featuring the restaurant's recipes. (*The Food for Thought Cookbook*
by Guy Garrett and Kit Norman, Thorsons Publishing Group,
1987).
   The main drawback at Food for Thought is the lack of space.
There are only 35 seats, which are extremely crammed together,
and this tends to make you feel rushed and hassled — rather
like eating on the 5.45 to Surbiton, albeit a rather trendy
Surbiton.
   The cheese used is not vegetarian, which is a pity.

Open: 12-8 Monday-Friday
Credits cards: none
Covent Garden tube
35 seats

Le Gourmet

312 King's Road, London SW3
☎ 01-352 4483
🏠 £12

I thought we had arrived in the middle of a party — but no, this is the regular atmosphere at Le Gourmet, and it's great either to observe or be part of. As soon as you open the door, Gus hails you from the other side of the restaurant and fits you in somewhere. An extraordinary banter about the food, the customers and Joan Collins is kept up for the rest of the meal.

There are three or four choices for vegetarians, and the main courses were tasty and the salad excellent.

Eating here is good fun and could be part of a special night out (do book), or go for a lazy Sunday lunch and take the papers. The cheese is non-vegetarian.

Open: 6.30-11.30 Monday-Saturday, 12.30-3, 6.30-11 Sunday
Sloane Square tube
62 seats

The Greenhouse

16 Chenies Street, London WC1
☎ 01-637 8038
£4.50

This is a busy basement restaurant that is pleasantly
unpretentious with simple decor, attractive pictures and plants,
whitewashed walls and a certain cosy, welcoming quality. I do
like this restaurant as the food looks and tastes good, the
portions are generous and the prices very reasonable.

There is a varying menu of wholesome savouries, pizza,
quiche, vegetable bakes and so on, as well as some tempting
cakes and puddings.

At times it can become extremely crowded and a little
oppressive — you may have to share a table and clear your own
space, and there could perhaps be a little more light by which
to see what you are eating.

The eggs are free-range but, sadly, the cheese is non-
vegetarian. Note that Monday evening from 6.30-9 is for women
only.

Open: 10-10 Monday-Friday, 1-10 Saturday
Credit cards: none
Goodge Street tube
50 seats

Inigo Jones

14 Garrick Street, London WC2
☎ 01-836 6456
🏠 £37.50

You certainly get vegetarian food with all the trimmings at Inigo
Jones, and service that is wonderfully attentive. The sommelier
wanders around with the traditional silver cup round his neck,
but you wouldn't expect anything less in a restaurant that has
so much style.

The set vegetarian meal costs £37.50, but it is six courses so,
although not cheap, it does seem good value for a really special
night out.

The menu does change. At the moment there is a pear and
watercress starter, followed by consommé with barley, a wild
mushroom tartlet, sorbet to clear the palate, then on again with
fresh herb ravioli, cheese selection and filled choux pastry
swans. If you didn't like the sound of any of the courses, I'm
sure they would be only too willing to make changes. The food
is not wholefood, nor is the cheese vegetarian.

Open: 12.30-2.30, 5.30-11.30 Monday-Friday, 5.30-11.30
        Saturday, closed Sunday
Covent Garden tube
70 seats

Jazz Café   ✓

56 Newington Green, London N16 9PX
☎ 01-359 4936
£7

Opened in 1987, described as a café, wine bar, vegetarian
restaurant and jazz venue.

The decor is smart but simple, with black tables and mesh
chairs, terrific lighting and the walls hung with an ever-changing
exhibition of prints or paintings.

The menu is displayed behind the bar; it is all vegetarian and
consists of fairly standard ideas, such as lasagne, moussaka or
cheesy vegetable bake, but they are very tasty and well-
presented, with a very fresh salad garnish. I had a subtle bean
and olive pâté for starters and couldn't resist a huge portion of
almond cake, which was very light and fragrant with lemon.

The prices are reasonable, not just for the food but the wines
too. We had an organic Muscadet, which was crisp and dry.

Unless you go early, it is advisable to book, as space is
limited. The music side of the Jazz Café has developed
considerably since the early days and there are now well-known
bands playing every night. As a result there is an admission
charge of £3 per head (or £2 if you are a student, unemployed
or a member of the Musicians' Union) in addition to your meal.
There is no charge at lunch-times though. Ask for a front table
if you are particularly interested in the music, otherwise sit in
the back section where you can still hear but needn't feel
overwhelmed.

My only worry for this place is that, because it is so small, it
will always be overcrowded. The ordering system at the bar is a
little annoying as you have to spend time queueing in the
middle of your meal if you decide to have a pudding. However,
there are obviously imaginative minds behind the venture and
these troubles will be sorted out.

Open: 12-3, 6.30-12 Monday-Saturday, 7-11 Sunday
Credit cards: none
73 or 30 bus
65 seats

🍾

Knoodles

30 Connaught Street, London W2
☎ 01-262 9623
🏠 £10

This was one of the early restaurants to specialize mainly in fresh pasta.

Sauces are all home-made and there are some interesting ones for vegetarians, such as the cultivated or wild mushroom sauce and stir-fry vegetables with Oriental sauce. To go with the sauces, there are five types of noodles to try — white, wholemeal, spinach, orange and tomato. There is also the house speciality called Knoodle Roll, which is a sheet of pasta, stuffed with spinach and cheese, rolled up and served with a rich tomato sauce. There are non-pasta choices, too: home-made soup (sometimes made with vegetable stock), Mozzarella cheese with fresh basil or baked garlic mushrooms.

I feel that the food here has a much more personal quality than most of the pasta chains and, as the non-vegetarian food is also interesting, it's a useful place to take mixed parties.

Open: 12-3, 6.30-10.45 for last orders Monday-Saturday
Marble Arch tube, then 15 bus
46 seats

Mandeer

21 Hanway Place, London W1
☎ 01-323 0660
🏠 £5 day, £12 evening

Situated in a labyrinthine basement in a rather seedy back street behind Tottenham Court Road, Mandeer is a surprise. One of the first completely vegetarian Indian restaurants in England, the decor is darkly oriental with great brass lamps.

There are two sections, a self-service canteen, which serves a variety of snacks and simple main courses at wonderfully cheap prices, and a regular, more formal restaurant with a full menu and waiter service. This is a good place for a pre-theatre meal or a night out.

There's a very good choice with some adventurous items, such as puffed lotus savoury, and tofu dishes. The portions are quite small for small for the price and the thali is probably a better bet for economy's sake. The wholemeal Indian breads are excellent. The puris arrive at the table puffed up and tasty.

Most of the sweets are milk-based, flavoured with sweet spices, brown sugar, saffron and nuts, but there are Himalayan apricots and fresh fruit for vegans.

The staff are very helpful with decisions when you are faced with a dauntingly large menu and, as you're given plenty of time, you can eat at leisure.

Open: 12-3, 5.45-10.30 Monday-Saturday
Tottenham Court Road tube
100 seats

Mildred's

58 Greek Street, London W1
☎ 01-494 1634
🏠 £5

This is an excellent, if somewhat small, wholefood café, much needed in the heart of Soho, that opened just before Christmas 1988.

The decor is simple, with plain walls and utilitarian, green Formica-topped tables, black wooden chairs and some more comfortable bench seating, but the soft paintwork and pretty vases of fresh flowers prevent it from being stark. The crowds that fill it at the peak lunch-time period make it very cosy.

The menu changes daily and during the day as well. There are usually two soups, occasionally a vegetarian pâté, three or four main courses and three puddings.

We had an excellent, rich, Hungarian mushroom soup with good wholemeal bread, followed by a colourful and crunchy stir-fry of vegetables and rice (minus the shrimp and cashew topping) and a tasty quiche, packed full of goodies, with a red bean salad. Others on our table consumed the chick pea curry and blueberry crumble with great relish.

The portions are generous and come simply served on plain, white, heavy china — and the food is piping hot too. There is table service, and, considering just two people were waiting on a full place, reasonably quick. However, if you want a more private meal, it would be worth avoiding the one o'clock rush hour. There is also a take-away service. Highly recommended.

Open: 11-10.30 Monday-Friday, 12-10.30 Saturday
Credit cards: none
34 seats

Millward's

97 Stoke Newington Church Street, London N16
☎ 01-254 1025
🏠 £8

Millward's has now established itself as a good and most popular place to eat. Booking is certainly advisable — the night I was there no fewer than 10 people were turned away.

The food is imaginative and well presented. The starters are displayed on the central bar, and every dish is served with a little garnish. The main course comes on a large plate with your choice of side-salad or selection of vegetables coming in a separate dish. We had a hefty nut and parsnip roast served with apple sauce, and a very good ravioli.

There were several appetizing puddings, too, and I couldn't resist a fresh fruit cheesecake, which was exceptionally light.

You can still try the 'tasty maisy' — a little bit of everything on the menu — which is a good idea for the sceptical diner or the fascinated quasi-vegetarian.

The restaurant is full of charming touches, like the well-cared for plants, interesting music and olives to nibble while you wait for your meal. As they are open 12 hours a day, you can go there for afternoon tea after a brisk walk round Clissold Park, which is just down the road, as well as for lunch or dinner.

Open: 12-12 daily
Credit cards: none
73 bus from Tottenham Court Road, 76 from city
42 seats

Neal's Yard Bakery and Tea Room

6 Neal's Yard, London WC2
☎ 01-836 5199
🏠 £4

Neal's Yard doesn't seem to change at all as the years go by!
You are still likely to get a seat under which next week's supply
of fruit juice is stacked, and they can certainly do nothing about
the lack of space. However, what does not change either is the
quality of the food. It is good and wholesome — nice, chewy
pizzas, well-made salads and tasty scones. They have a range of
excellent cakes, some vegan and others sugar-free.

Neal's Yard really works best as a take-away, as it is extremely
crowded at meal times. If you do manage to penetrate the
upstairs tea room, then the choice of herb teas is excellent and
all are served in homely brown tea pots.

Lunch starts at noon and, on the evenings when they are open
late, there is a separate menu from 5.30. The prices are very
reasonable for such good-quality food.

The eggs used are free-range, but the cheese isn't necessarily
vegetarian. There is also a small vegetarian take-away food bar
on the opposite side of the Yard.

Open: 10.30-7.30 Monday and Tuesday, closed Wednesday,
       10.30-7.30 Thursday and Friday, 10.30-4.30 Saturday,
       closed Sunday
Credit cards: none
Covent Garden tube
20 seats

Plummers

33 King Street, London WC2
☎ 01-240 2534
🏠 £12

Martin Plummer, the owner, makes sure there is always a choice of three main courses for vegetarians that are guaranteed not to contain animal fats or meat products.

The standard main courses are a pie with a good chunky filling, a casserole and a cream cheese and spinach crumble.

The atmosphere is pleasant: Laura Ashley and muted Victorian decor with efficient and attentive service (12½ per cent). A good place for a business lunch, a night out, or a meal before the theatre or cinema.

The ice-cream is Loseley and therefore safe, but the cheese is non-vegetarian.

Open: 12.20-2.30, 6-11.30 Monday to Friday, 6-11.30 Saturday
Covent Garden tube
80 seats

Quaffers

8 Norfolk Place, London W2
☎ 01-724 6046
🍷 £12

Quaffers is the kind of wine bar everyone would like to have close by with its pleasant decor, warm welcome, helpful staff, and a good choice of well-prepared vegetarian dishes at a very affordable price.

The menu changes daily, but a permanent fixture by popular demand is the deep-fried potato skins, which are terrific. Other starters include soups made with vegetable stocks, crudités and mushroom stuffed with cream cheese.

Regular main courses include pancakes, mushroom Stroganov or an exotic fruit, nut and cottage cheese salad. There are always a few daily specials and hot dishes are served with at least four vegetables.

The desserts are imaginative, too, with home-made cheesecakes, apple and sultana crumble or hot brandy bananas.

Open: 12-2.30, 5.30-11.30 Monday-Friday, 5.30-11.30
       Saturday, closed Sunday
Paddington tube
45 seats

Rani

3-5 Long Lane, London N3
☎ 01-349 4386
🏠 £7

Rani is recently expanded and decorated in a cheerful, modern style, serving excellent Bombay-style food. The cooking, by the women of the Brahmin family, who own the restaurant, is delicate and subtly spiced.

The papadoms — plain or fiery — come folded, the dal cakes with a wonderful coconut chutney, paper thin dosas with a tasty sauce, and the most delicious savoury rice.

There are also some most imaginative dishes on the menu. I tried the odd-sounding banana methi, a combination of spinach and banana with fenugreek leaves which was simply terrific. Apart from the choices on the menu there are different daily specials, such as stuffed aubergines and potato curry on Wednesday with Al Tiki with tamarind and yoghurt sauce as a starter, and stuffed green chilli bhaji on Saturdays.

The service is discreet and friendly and the whole evening out doesn't cost an arm and a leg. Rani sets out to give you delicious food in unpretentious style and it certainly achieves this. Highly recommended.

Open: 6-12 Monday and Tuesday, 12-3, 6-12 Wednesday-
       Sunday
Finchley Central tube
30 seats

Seasons

22 Harcourt Street, London W1
☎ 01-402 5925
🏠£5

Seasons has a nice fresh feel to it, and not just because it was opened as recently as Christmas 1988. The decor is plain white, with white chairs and marble topped tables on a wood floor. Fresh flowers and colourful pictures plus good lighting give it an attractive ambiance.

The ground floor section, with 16 seats, is non-smoking, and also where the open plan kitchen is situated. Downstairs, the main body of the restaurant is surprisingly light and airy because of the mirrored walls.

The menu is quite simple with a choice of humus or soup as starters. When I went the soup was an interesting combination of spinach and coconut. There is a hot main course, such as sweet-and-sour vegetables with rice, as well as the more predictable quiche. The choice of salads was excellent. All looked extremely fresh, and there were good mixtures, such as red cabbage with beans, Waldorf with cauliflower in a creamy dressing, amongst the five available. These can be had as a salad platter or as single portions.

The puddings consisted of fruit fools, crumble or carrot and cinnamon cake.

The menu varies each day, and they intend to expand the choice according to demand. 'Service with a smile' is part of their advertisement, and, certainly, I found the staff very friendly.

Open: 10.30-10 Monday-Saturday, 10.30-6.30 Sunday
Edgware Road tube
40 seats
 day; ⬛evening ⊘ section

Shahanshah

60 North Road, Southall, London
☎ 01-574 1493
🏠 £4

A pure Indian vegetarian restaurant in the heart of Southall that mainly caters for take-aways — but has 20 seats and counter service.

The food here is authentic, absolutely delicious and still incredibly cheap. The samosas, a speciality of the place, are huge, crisp, spicy and the bhaluka (fluffy, puffy, spiced bread with a crisp outside) are amazing. The range of sweets is enormous and the carrot halva is light, moist, scented and sweet. You can gorge yourself well and truly for under £4.

It certainly deserves praise for the truly excellent food and value.

Their other branch is at 17 South Road, Southall and it is closed on Wednesdays. If you are making a special trip, try to check. They also cater for weddings and tea parties.

Open: 10-8 Monday, closed Tuesday, 10-8 Wednesday-Sunday
Credit cards: none
Southall BR
20 seats

&

Veeraswamy's

99-101 Regent Street, London W1
☎ 01-734 1401
🏠 £15

Veeraswamy's was opened in 1922, so it has claim to being the oldest Indian restaurant in London.

The setting is very sumptuous, luxurious and very, very Indian. The whole experience begins when you meet the costumed lift attendant who ushers you upstairs. The staff are very friendly and attentive and only too willing to explain about the food.

There is a good choice for vegetarians. The mint paratha was unusual, the panir makhri had a delicious, fragrant sauce. Vegetable kofta are light dumpling-like balls of fried vegetables with a hot spicy sauce. Everything was well presented.

To follow, one of the more unusual desserts on offer was a tamarind sorbet with a distinct sweet-and-sour taste. The more classic Indian puddings are also available.

Veeraswamy's is certainly the place to go for a stylish night out, especially for parties with mixed eating habits. Most of the vegetarian dishes are cheaper.

Open: 11.30-3, 6.30-12 daily
Piccadilly Circus tube
80 seats

The Windmill

486 Fulham Road, London SW6
 01-385 1570
£6

The Windmill is a cheerful and very informal restaurant.

The food is always imaginatively prepared, tastefully presented and delicious. There is a frequently changing choice, all fully described so you can tell exactly what is vegan or what has been organically grown.

There's a wonderful range of fresh-looking salads and tempting puddings — I couldn't resist a rich carob and butterscotch flan. The portions are good and the meals here are excellent value.

Being so small, The Windmill soon gets full and has little space for queuing, but it is worth the hassle. The surroundings are not especially comfortable — PVC tablecloths and hard chairs — but they do put candles on the tables in the evenings to create an atmosphere.

It is a good place for a casual night out, and somewhere you could feel happy eating on your own.

The eggs are free-range and the cheese vegetarian. They sell organic wine.

Open: 12-11 Monday-Saturday, 7-11 Sunday
Credit cards: none
Fulham Broadway tube
28 seats

Woodlands

77 Marylebone Lane, London, W1
 01-486 3862
£10

This excellent chain of restaurants reaches from Delhi through
London to New York, serving the now familiar Bombay cuisine.
The dishes taste individually spiced and are prepared by expert
chefs from India.

There's a very wide choice of pancakes, dosas and different
rice dishes. The Royal Thali is a sumptuous feast with delicate
samosas and the lassi with saffron and almond is luscious.

The food is pricey compared with other bhelpoori houses,
justified perhaps by the impeccable service and luxurious
surroundings. All three restaurants are highly recommended, as
is the food which is consistently excellent.

OTHER BRANCHES AT:
37 Panton Street, London SW1
    01-839 7258
402 High Road, Wembley, Middlesex
    01-902 9869

Open: 12-3, 6-11 daily
Bond Street tube
120 seats

Zen

Chelsea Cloisters, London SW3
 01-589 1781
£15

It's nice to eat good vegetarian food in plush, spacious and comfortable surroundings.

There is a page on the menu of vegetarian dishes, which confusingly includes a fish dish. However, there was certainly no muddle about the food we ordered. It was all beautifully presented in delicate portions, leaving you room to get through a lot of different dishes. There were tiny spring rolls with chilli sauce, crisply-fried sweet and sour seaweed, and minute parcels of tofu, stuffed with fragrantly spiced vegetables.

When you are feeling adventurous, try some of the more unusual puddings such as the sago and melon dessert. To my surprise it was delicious, light and refreshing.

The same management own I Ching, which also offers a range of vegetarian dishes.

Open: 12-3, 6-11 Monday-Friday, 12-11.30 Saturday
South Kensington tube
150 seats

Zzzzz's

238 Gray's Inn Road, London WC1
☎ 01-278 5391
🏠 £3

This deservedly popular vegetarian take-away is a good place for tasty filling lunches.

You can choose from freshly-filled baps, and an interesting selection of eight or more salads, including imaginative combinations such as wheatberry or broccoli and seaweed. There are jacket potatoes, soup, and tremendous wholemeal quiches packed with different vegetables, nuts, seeds and sometimes chewy cheese topping.

The cakes and puddings are also a great temptation and their crumble is excellent.

There is a minimum charge of £1.75 from 12-2.

Open: 8.30-3.30 Monday-Saturday
Credit cards: none
King's Cross, Chancery Lane tube
27 seats

South East
Kent, Surrey, Sussex

There are several strictly vegetarian places in this region, all of which have a strong commitment and an imaginative approach to the food. It is possible to eat in comfort and style at places like Barts and Hockneys, which are the highlights in the South. In fact, both these restaurants are easily accessible to Londoners and well worth the drive out.

More casual eating, just as well presented, is to be had at Brants and Food for Friends. These are in the seaside towns of Hastings and Brighton respectively, but most of the other coastline towns have little in the way of good vegetarian food, which is surprising considering the numbers and types of visitors who must surely expect more than fish chips and burgers.

In the rest of the region, most of the other places reviewed offer mixed fare, and a mixture of standards. There is a reasonable choice of pubs, smarter restaurants and basic in-town cafés.

Alfresco

45 Bouverie Road West, Folkestone, Kent, CT20 2SZ
☎ 0303 43831
🏠 £6

This is a fairly new restaurant, the staff are very keen and the food very good!

Although it is relaxed and friendly, Alfresco gives a meal there a sense of occasion and makes it all seem like a treat, which indeed it was.

The choice for vegetarians is small, but they are very willing to leave meat out of certain dishes to give you more of a choice if you ask. The food was all beautifully presented.

We had the three mushroom and leek soup, which was delicious and very well flavoured. The deep-fried Lymeswold, served with tangy gooseberry sauce was an unusual idea that worked, but, be warned, it is quite rich.

Apart from the vegetable and pasta *gratin*, there is a daily 'Hot special', such as lentil loaf. This is served with seasonal vegetables or French bread.

The desserts are of the calorific variety with gâteaux, such as orange and almond or coffee and walnut, and some special ice-creams and sorbets. The whole menu changes slightly monthly.

Apart from serving lunches, Alfresco is open as a café throughout the day serving croissant and pastries, with a good choice of hot and cold drinks and on Friday and Saturday evenings.

As you would expect from the name, the decor is fresh and reminiscent of picnics, with bright wall paintings, and startling green undercloths for the tables, over which are starched, white linen table-cloths.

Open: Monday-Thursday, 10-5, 7-10.30 Friday and Saturday
60 seats
 section

Bart's

34 The Street, Ashtead, Surrey, KT21 2AH
☎0372 275491
🏠£9

Be careful not to blink as you drive through Ashtead otherwise
you'll miss Bart's. Although it is on the main road, it is tucked
into a bend and heavily disguised as a suburban semi! Once
inside, this impression is quickly forgotten as you discover a
charming, elegant little restaurant.

The tables are well spaced, the chairs comfortable and the
decor simple, painted in warm tones of peach and grey. There
are fresh flowers on the tables and pretty lighting. On the walls
are a few original collage pictures plus a portrait of Bart the dog,
after whom the place is named.

The food is quite simple with a choice of three or four starters,
including a very good soup and home-made roll. The main
courses have been different each time I've been as the menu is
changed frequently. It is exclusively wholefood, though certainly
not heavy, and no frozen food is used. There is usually a quiche
served with a good, unusual salad platter that might have
buckwheat, pumpkin seeds or even seaweed amongst the
greenery. Hot main courses might include risottos, lasagne or
hazelnut roast. These are always well presented and come with a
separate side-salad rather than hot vegetables.

Their home-made ice-creams, such as malt and carob, are
excellent, and in summer there are good, fresh fruit tarts and
some imaginative desserts, such as peach fool made with tofu.
You would never guess!

Dinner at Bart's is a delight. The service is friendly and
efficient, and you're encouraged to spend time enjoying the meal
and the pleasant surroundings. The place is immaculate, and if
you peek into the kitchens on your way to the loo you will find
them spotless too. That in itself is a very high recommendation.

It is very unusual to find anywhere in the home counties
where you can, as a vegetarian, dine in some style and comfort.
It has the added advantage that it will also charm carnivores.

Open: 12-2, 7-10 Tuesday-Friday, 7-10 Saturday
Credit cards: none
20 seats

♿ 🍼 📋 🚭

43

Brants

45 High Street, Old Town, Hastings, TN34 3EW
0424 431896
£3

Brants is in the old part of Hastings, up an interesting little
street that, as the name implies, must once have been the town
centre. Beware the surrounding antique shops: I was tempted in
and came home from my visit to Hastings with more than I had
intended!

There has been a vegetarian restaurant on this site for nearly
20 years, which must be a record. The present owners have
been there about four years and they run it well with everything
neat and clean. The decor is simple with pine tables and a small
counter where you can see most of the food on display.

They open for coffee and serve an excellent range of cakes,
scones and slices. I had a delicious raspberry bun.

At lunch there's a choice of salads, quiche, nut savoury and a
couple of 'Hot specials', such as lasagne or vegetable *gratin*. The
service is quick and efficient, and the prices very reasonable.

In the summer, eaters can spill out into the little walled
garden behind. It is a terrific sun trap, or at least was the day
we were there. You can listen to the gulls and feel quite at the
seaside, with the added advantage of being away from the
crowds. I also bet that this little restaurant is good in the winter!

Open: 10-5 Monday-Saturday, til 2 Wednesday, in summer,
       10-2.30 Monday-Saturday, closed Wednesday in winter
Credit cards: none
30 seats

Burdocks

59 High Street, Billingshurst, West Sussex, RH12 9QP
☎ 0403 812750
£6

The restaurant is in a very attractive building with low beams, huge fireplace and stone floor. Billingshurst is a pretty village in the heart of some lovely Sussex countryside. I'm perhaps somewhat biased as I was born in a little village close by!

We went here for Sunday lunch, surrounded by roast-beef-and-Yorkshire-pudding-eaters, and were told that we were the first to ask for the vegetarian dish of the day! Still, at least the option is there, and it is possibly a more popular choice mid week, especially as the same dish is a little cheaper then.

There is only the one dish. It might be spinach pancakes, vegetable charlotte, peanut loaf, haricot casserole and so on. When we went there was a version of pasta and tomato sauce. It arrived served in an individual bowl with an attractive side-salad and was piping hot. The portion was rather small, but what there was was very tasty.

For pudding there were some lovely home-made treats of treacle tart and lemon meringue pie. We had a sharp, blackcurrant crumble with cream. As everything is made on the premises it is easy to check on the ingredients, as I did, so that you can enjoy your food despite the predominance of meat.

Apart from lunch, during the rest of the day they serve good tea, coffee and a wide selection of home-made cakes, sandwiches and biscuits.

Open: 9.30-5 Tuesday-Saturday, 12-5 Sunday

Credit cards: none
28 seats
♿ 🍾 📓 🚭 section

Clinch's Salad House

14 Southgate, Chichester, PO19 1ES
☎ 0243 788822
🏠 £4

As the name implies, there's a plentiful choice of salads here —
as many as eight if you arrive early enough for the full selection.
They are fairly standard combinations but well prepared and
fresh to look at. They use a variety of beans, yellow and green
split peas, wheat, rice, beansprouts and plenty of fresh, seasonal
vegetables.

There's also a choice of hot dishes, such as nut roast,
ratatouille, moussaka or macaroni cheese and, to follow, lots of
home-made sweets. Everything is made on the premises so it's
easy to check if the cheesecake has gelatine in it, for example
and the staff are very willing to assist you.

Clinch's is also a nice place to go in the afternoon as there are
cakes and some particularly good, if rather sweet, biscuits.

The restaurant is divided into several different areas and we
sat in a pretty conservatory room, which was most comfortable
and quiet.

Open: 8-5.30 Monday-Saturday
Credit cards: none
42 seats
🍾 🍽 🚭 section

46

Cornerstone

25a High Street, Ashford, Kent, TN24 8TH
☎0233 42874
🏠£4

This is a very pleasant coffee bar and café, serving a lovely range of vegetarian food. Everyone who works here, including those in the craft and bookshop downstairs, is a committed Christian. There's a leaflet describing their *raison d'être* and the staff will enter into discussion with you if you want to but apart from that there's no bible thumping at all.

The food is good nicely cooked, well flavoured and served in ample portions. The menu is small with three choices of main course, such as lentil curry with rice, nut roast and salad, or stuffed marrow. The selection of 'Hot specials' changes daily. Lighter snacks of soup with home-baked bread, and jacket potatoes are also available. The salads were very crisp and fresh and the mixtures included a colourful red cabbage and peanut coleslaw and a rich Waldorf with celery, sultanas and apple. On the tables are a very good vinaigrette, and a lovely home-made herbed mayonnaise.

The prices here are good, the place is clean and comfortable and the staff are friendly. Cornerstone is certainly good value for wholesome, day-time eating.

Open: 10-5.30 Tuesday-Saturday
Credit cards: none
45 seats

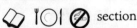 section

The Courtyard

6 East Street, Tonbridge, Kent, TN9 1HG
☎ 0732 359973
🏠 £8

This attractive restaurant is just off the main street in Tonbridge.
There is no street parking but there are some spaces in a road
behind the near-by Tonbridge Parish Church. Then it's a short
walk through the church grounds, past some lovely old red brick
buildings.

The entrance to the restaurant is, in effect, a courtyard, but it
is covered over by the most prolific vine. This cool, leafy area
forms a small bar where you can sit and order your meal. The
restaurant is prettily decorated in shades of pink, with dark
wooden tables set with attractive tableware.

My starter of tropical fruit salad was a mixture of avocado,
banana, mango and grapes, all painstakingly laid out on the
plate. I thought the portion was a little on the meagre side, but
this was perhaps a good thing considering the huge quantity of
nut roast that came as the main course. It was a mixture of
finely chopped walnuts and vegetables, which kept the texture
light and moist, and so tasty that it was impossible to leave
any!

Other main courses were a rich mushroom Stroganoff, leek
and cheese pancakes, and ratatouille lasagne.

The side-salad was quite plain and the vegetables
disappointingly over-cooked.

For dessert you select from a traditional sweet trolley. There
are also hot pancakes and a good selection of ice-creams,
sorbets and sundaes.

The friendly service and attractive surroundings make this a
very acceptable place for an evening out, especially for parties of
mixed eating preferences. At the moment the menu is likely to
stay the same for some months, but I'm sure regulars here could
encourage variety.

Open: 12-2, 6.30-9.30 Monday-Friday, 12-2, 6.30-10 Saturday,
12-2 Sunday
40 seats

Dodgers Restaurant

55 High Street, Rochester, Kent, ME1 1LN
☎ 0634 408077
🏠 £8

Don't let the fact that this is an American hamburger joint put you off. The owner here is very enthusiastic about adding vegetarian food to his menu and wouldn't mind a stampede of vegetarians through his door!

Starters are limited to melon, or soup (do check on the stock).

On the main course menu there was a very good asparagus quiche, served with jacket potato (or chips) and a salad, or a daily 'Hot special', which is well prepared even though it is likely to be something not very much out of the ordinary, such as aubergine lasagne. This also comes with a jacket potato and salad. There are also other pasta dishes, such as mushroom fettucine. The portions are *huge*!

The menu is made up of some rather poor puns about cars: the meat dishes are listed under the heading 'Major Overhaul', while the vegetarian repertoire fares rather better under the title 'Special Tune Up' (try to ignore the fact that a ham salad is listed in this section).

Lots of clutter, gingham table-cloths and a big wooden bar all contribute to a very good atmosphere. The service is slick. Although it would not be to everyone's taste, it is good for a night out with a crowd.

Open: 10-2.15, 7-10 Tuesday-Sunday
80 seats

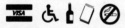

Food For Friends

Prince Albert Street, Brighton, East Sussex
☎0273 202310
£6

A deservedly busy and very popular restaurant that really shows
how imaginative a small menu can be, and how well a small
serving area can be operated. Although there doesn't appear to
be much choice, everything sounds very tempting.

The food on offer is the same throughout the day and follows
what is evidently a well-tried formula. There is always soup and
home-made bread, a couple of 'Hot specials', such as Mexican
tortilla bake, or Shanghai spring rolls, quiche, and a choice of
salads with the option of two dressings, such as mushroom and
red wine, or blue cheese and sour cream. Dressings are extra on
the bill. They always try to make the soup vegan, plus one 'Hot
special' dish and a dressing.

The puddings follow the same lines — one hot, one cold,
using seasonal fruit where possible.

The style is very straightforward: read the blackboard, decide
what you want, order, pay, grab your cutlery and find
somewhere to sit.

The no-frills, no-nonsense approach extends to both the
service, which is efficient to the point of being abrupt, and the
decor, which is plain with pine tables, plants and not too much
space. The turnover of people is quick and the tables are cleared
frequently. At busy times you'll have to share, though no one
rushes you away.

Food For Friends certainly isn't the place for an intimate
dinner or leisurely lunch, but it is excellent for casual eating
throughout the day and a good place to bring non-vegetarian
sceptics who still think we live on brown rice and rabbit food.

Open: 9-10 Monday-Friday, til 11 Saturday, 10-10 Sunday
60 seats

Food for Living

116 High Street, Chatham, Kent, ME4 4BY
☎ 0634 409 291
🏠 £3

This is a cheap and cheerful little café, linked with a wholefood shop, with significantly more to offer than the usual fast food quiche-caterers.

The main hot dish of the day is available between 12 and 2.30, otherwise there are pizzas (vegan or vegetarian) tartex sandwiches, savoury flan and jacket potatoes.

The selection of wholemeal cakes was particularly good with carrot cake, carob and peanut flapjack or carob and coconut wedge.

Although it is nothing really special, Food for Living is a welcome eatery in an otherwise typical modern shopping centre.

Open: 9-4.30 Monday-Saturday
Credit cards: none
40 seats

Henty Arms

2 Ferring Lane, Ferring, West Sussex, BN12 6QY
☎ 0903 41254
🏠 £5 bar, £11 restaurant

The Henty Arms is a typical, cosy, village pub with a rather
adventurous landlady who is building up a substantial
vegetarian menu of home-made dishes.

All week there are at least three bar snack choices, including
cashew and walnut risotto, nut roast, fettucine and, sometimes,
stuffed vine leaves.

On Thursday nights there is a special four-course vegetarian
meal, served in the restaurant, for an all-inclusive price of
£10.50. There is a choice of three starters, such as pâté and
soup, and four or five main courses. These include wholesome
dishes, such as bean and lentil casserole, or lasagne, some of
which are also suitable for vegans.

It is very encouraging to see this food becoming standard in a
pub.

Open: 12-2, 6.30-9.30 daily
bar 30, restaurant 26 seats

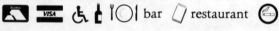 bar restaurant

Hockney's

98 High Street, Croydon
☎ 01-688 8624
🏠 £8

'The food works on the principle that you don't have to suffer
when eating vegetarian', says the publicity blurb in the hand-out
describing the Arts Centre which houses Hockney's restaurant,
and it's certainly true. It's a most pleasant place with an
excellent and imaginative menu. The restaurant is upstairs and
consists of a large, open room, brightly decorated. There's a
spacious, airy feeling with plenty of room between the tables
and good lighting. The menu includes ideas from different
cuisines such as Mexican, Greek and Malaysian. They make
some very imaginative meals too. I had the 'Peacock Pie' which
consisted of a layer of onion, black eye beans, cashews and
creamed coconut, covered with a topping of puréed cauliflower,
tomato and cheese. Delicious! The puddings consist of home-
made ice-cream, parfaits and concoctions made with fruit salad,
as well as a choice of cakes.

Open: 12-10.30 Tuesday-Saturday
80 seats

Holland and Barrett

12 Station Parade, Eastbourne, BN21 1BE
☎ 0323 28508
🏠 £3

Don't be put off if it's a struggle getting in here! The congestion is partly caused by the position of the serving area. It is right up by the entrance door which, being at the top of a flight of stairs, makes it hard to know where to queue. The service is a little slow too, so a jam tends to form.

At this Holland and Barrett, there is a fairly ordinary menu, but the choice is good and it is reasonably priced. I had a small mixed salad, which was a substantial meal as it consisted of six different salads piled into quite a large bowl. The hot dish of the day varies. When I went it was a tasty spinach roulade. Occasionally you may find that the 'Hot special' is vegan. There were some mouthwatering pasties on display, and also quiche and soup. There are also all the usual juices, teas, coffees, cakes and sundries.

For those of you who want to eat early, they are also doing a breakfast menu with 'cereal, grapefruit and things on toast', and, for the health-conscious, they offer a choice between skimmed and full-fat milk.

The restaurant itself is furnished in a plain style with simple seating in three different rooms — all quite airy — and an upstairs area that is non-smoking.

The restaurant is pleasant enough, but it is not very memorable. Sadly there is little in Eastbourne for the vegetarian wanting to dine out. I was directed to one awful place where I could just make out some cauliflower cheese lurking amongst slabs of meat. I beat a hasty retreat. Perhaps there is an opportunity here for some enterprising folk as I'm sure there must be the demand.

Open: 9.30-4.30 Monday-Saturday
Credit cards: none
60 seats

🍽️ ⊘ section

Loseley House

Loseley Park, Guildford, Surrey, GU3 1HS
☎ 04833 571881
🏠 £4

Loseley Park is just outside Guildford on the A3100. The restaurant is in an old tithe barn, set in the midst of farmland. It is the cows that graze here which produce the milk for the Loseley range of dairy products.

Although the vegetarian menu is a little limited, I felt this place was worth a mention as so much of what is on sale here uses the farm products as well as organic vegetables and flour whenever possible, and free-range eggs.

Of the starters, the soup is usually suitable for vegetarians (though do just check when you go) and there's a choice of several quiches. I had a delicious tomato, courgette and pepper one served hot and there were two other types served cold. These come with a standard side-salad. Jacket potato and salad, and egg mayonnaise were also on the menu. Some of you may be put off by the slices of cold meat and ham on the table with the quiches.

There are generally three or four cakes and several biscuits on sale.

The food is served on nice pottery and the service is of the 'pick and get helped to it' variety, which can get a little slow when a queue builds up.

Loseley House offers more than just food, however. The Elizabethan House is worth a visit and, at the farm shop, you can buy a good selection of organic vegetables, bread, cakes and all the Loseley products.

Open: 12-5 daily from Whit Monday-end September
Credit cards: none
100 seats

♿ 🍽 ⊖

The Old Neptune

Marine Terrace, Whitstable, Kent, CT5 1EJ
☎ 0227 272262
🏠 £2

It is not often that I recommend a place selling chips — even if
they are supposed to be the best in Whitstable! However, they
are ideal with the fabulous American-style vegeburgers on sale
here. The burgers are huge and crammed with lettuce, tomato,
onion and cucumber, plus garlic mayonnaise. Cheese and
pineapple can be added for a little extra. Apart from this
paradoxically wholesome 'junk food', there are salad platters
with cheese or cottage cheese, or filled jacket potatoes on the
menu at this seaside pub.

The location is lovely and you'll feel less guilty indulging in
this wicked meal if you take advantage of some of the
marvellous coastal walks that are within easy reach of here.

Open: 11-11 Monday-Saturday, 12-3, 7-10.30 Sunday
Credit cards: none
50 seats

♿ 🍷 📄 🚭

Pilgrims

37 Mount Ephraim, Tunbridge Wells, Kent, TN4 8AA
☎ 0892 20121
🏠 £5

Pilgrims Restaurant is to be found behind a well-stocked healthfood shop a little way out of the centre of Tunbridge Wells. The seating area is very pleasant with light wooden furniture, separated by wide troughs filled with plants, giving a greenhouse look to the whole room. Sadly the effect is somewhat spoilt by the very modern, canteen-style serving counter. However, it does mean you can slide your tray along, cope with your shopping *and* see the food clearly. In the cold compartment in the first part of the counter there is a good range of salads, served with savoury quiche. For hot meals there is usually a choice of two main courses, such as aubergine savoury or haricot bean *provencale*, but it's not all wholefood, as was evident in the cakes and slices at the end, which could mostly be described as gooey. There are the usual range of hot and cold drinks.

It was a little late for lunch so there was a limited amount of food left and I did not get the impression that anyone was going to put themselves out to see if anything could be rustled up. So get there early to ensure you have a choice.

One good idea from Pilgrims is their early evening opening. Many restaurants attached to a shop tend not to open because the shop needs to be staffed too, but at Pilgrims the shop stays open. This means you can have a decent supper out *and* do your week's shopping in one trip.

Open: 9-4 Monday, 9-8 Tuesday-Saturday
Credit cards: none
44 seats
 section

58

Poppies Coffee Shop and Restaurant

165 Montague Street, Worthing, West Sussex, BN11 3BZ
☎ 0903 31132
 £5.

This homely little restaurant is very suitable for an everyday vegetarian lunch, snack or afternoon tea. The staff are young and very friendly and come to your table to take your order. The regulars seem to prefer this to the usual self-service style which seems to be the norm for so many other similar places.

All the usual items are to be had: savoury quiche, choice of salads, and appetizing sandwiches with salad garnish.

There were a number of cakes to choose from, including two sorts of doughnuts, and plenty of different drinks. Interestingly the topping on the cheesecake was sugar-free.

A wholefood restaurant has been on this site for some time, but was renamed Poppies when it was taken over a year or so ago.

Open: 9.30-5.30 Winter (closed Sunday); 9.30-7.00 Summer
Credit cards: none
28 seats

⌐ ⃠ section

59

Riverside Restaurant

136 South Street, Lewes, East Sussex, BN7 2BS
☎ 0273 471018
🏠 £9

There is an appropriately boaty feel to the Riverside Restaurant with nets and green glass balls festooning the walls. It is wonderful to sit in the conservatory at the back and gaze over the river and the Downs. The ventilation isn't too good, though, and sadly the place gets a little smoky by mid evening.

Sue and Tim, the proprietors, are very cheery and enthusiastic. Apparently, being boat enthusiasts, they go up by river to do their shopping.

The menu is inventive, half the starters and half the main courses are vegetarian (some of these are also vegan) and the remaining food is fish. There are usually two or three starters, such as soup, pâté and crudites, and several main courses. We had the choice of vegetable paella, or chilli beans with saffron rice, layered mange-tout and vegetable cutlets, and vegetable pie (the pastry was excellent, crisp and nutty). This menu changes every three to four weeks, and Sue is particularly keen to introduce new ideas.

The puds are quite traditional with fruit pies, ice-cream and carrot cake.

Since we visited, they have decided to make the riverside terrace into a non-smoking area, so I think it will be an even nicer place for an agreeable evening out.

Open: 12-2, 7-9.30 Wednesday-Saturday,
        12-2 Sunday in summer, closed in winter
30 seats
▨ 🍷 ⧄ 🚭 section

60

The Rose and Crown

Fletching Street, Mayfield, East Sussex, TN20 6TE
☎ 0435 872200
🏠 £5

I was lucky enough to visit this delightful pub on a summer
day, and so sat outside in the delightful rambling garden. The
food was enjoyable too, despite the fact that, when we went, the
owners (one of whom supervises the catering side) were on
holiday.

There are usually about four choices suitable for vegetarians —
all quite standard stuff, such as cheese and onion pasty,
vegetable pie, tagliatelle — but the pastry and pasta is usually
wholemeal. The portions are very generous and come with a
side-salad or a good range of hot vegetables. The chap who
brought the food to our table was quite willing to nip back to
the kitchen and check our roast potatoes had been done in
vegetable oil too.

The range of starters is more limited. Occasionally there is a
vegetable soup, but more often it contains chicken stock, and in
the summer there might be seasonal fruit.

Puddings are of the traditional and sticky variety with banofie
pie, crumbles, and, again, more use of fresh fruits in the
summer.

Most of the food here is cooked on the premises, so if you
aren't sure about anything you can easily find out.

The Rose and Crown is certainly a delightful place to go for
lunch, or in the evening for a pub meal, and the surrounding
countryside is lovely. It is possible to book tables in their small
dining room where the same food is served.

The Rose and Crown is within easy reach of Tunbridge Wells.

Open: 12-2, 7-9 Sunday and Monday, 12-2, 7-9.30 Tuesday,
        12-2, 7-10 Wednesday-Saturday
Credit cards: none
22 seats in dining room

Russet Restaurant

34 King Street, Maidstone, Kent, NE14 1BS
☎ 0622 53921
🏠 £3

Russet is a typical high street Saturday shopping-type of place that is to be applauded for making the effort to include a small vegetarian selection in amongst the fish and beefburgers.

Hot dishes, including ratatouille with garlic bread, vegetable quiche with salad, and daily specials, such as ravioli with tomato sauce, are chalked up on the blackboard.

It is a pleasant place to eat. The decor is cream, with contrasting dark wood tables and bentwood chairs. Russet has a good local clientele and perhaps if a few more vegetarians venture in they may gradually expand the scope and imagination of the menu for us.

Open: 9-5.30 Monday-Saturday
Credit cards: none
50 seats

♿ 🍶 📖 🚬

St Martins Tea Rooms

3 St Martins Street, Chichester, West Sussex, PO19 1NP
☎ 0243 786715
 £5

The quality of the food is of prime importance to the owners of St Martins Tea Rooms. They use nothing containing preservatives, colourings or added flavourings, and in nine years have only opened *one* tin and think that was a mistake.

The menu isn't completely vegetarian, but there is quite a choice for vegetarians. You would be a bit pushed for choice though if you are vegan.

They make all their own soup using vegetable stock, as the meat stock goes off too quickly. For more substantial lunches there are cottage cheese open sandwiches, a special recipe Welsh rarebit and usually a vegetarian quiche. The 'Hot special' changes daily. When I visited it was vegetable fricassee with cheese sauce.

St Martins Tea Rooms make some delicious cakes with organic flour and try to keep the cholesterol level down by using sunflower or olive oil. Most things are on display at the serving bar or described on the blackboard. Once you order, the food is brought to your table.

The Tea Rooms are quite darkly furnished with traditional-style oak tables. I imagine it would be delightfully cosy in winter, and in the summer, there is a lovely garden to sit in.

Open: 10-6 Tuesday-Saturday
Credit cards: none
70 seats plus garden

🍾 ▯ 🚭

Seasons

12a Fisher Street, Lewes, East Sussex, BN7 2OP
☎ 0273 479279
£3 day, £6 evening

This is a plain and simple café with a straightforward,
wholefood, vegetarian menu. Everything is home-made and the
prices are reasonable.

During the day there are soups and basic starters, such as
humus and egg mayonnaise, plus many snack-style savouries —
sandwiches, flans, and a variety of cakes.

In the evenings the menu is a little more extensive and they
offer a set three-course meal for £6, which includes a choice of
two starters and four main courses. These include such dishes
as *croustade*, cottage pie, lasagne and the like. They are served
with hot, fresh vegetables or a salad.

Seasons is a good palce to quell a rumbling stomach in the
day, and for supper when you don't want to bother making your
own. Smoking is allowed but discouraged.

Open: 11-3 Monday-Thursday, 11-3, 6.30-9.30 Friday,
      6.30-9.30 Saturday (bookings only Friday and Saturday)
Credit cards: none
36 seats

       ♿ ⦿ day ▱ evening ☕

Under the Clock

51 High Street, Rochester, Kent, ME1 1LN
☎ 0634 42178
🏠 £9

There is a drawing-room feel to this cosy restaurant with its pale green walls, plain, dark-wood tables, candles and intimate atmosphere. The present owners took over in 1988 and they are trying to build up a more extensive vegetarian menu, so it will be interesting to watch developments.

The food we had was good and herbs and flavourings were used well, but what was lacking was presentation. The eggs mexicaine we had seemed at first to be a mountain of rice (white), smothered in tomato and pepper sauce, which, initially, was very off-putting. Other choices were lasagne or hot-pot, risotto with basil and tomatoes, or cheese pie with potatoes. Starters included stuffed mushrooms, or melon with port.

The portions were ample and we certainly left satisfied, though a little deafened by the loud music coming from the wine bar in the basement.

Open: 12-2, 7-10 daily, except Tuesday
12 seats
 section

Southern

Dorset, Hampshire

This part of Britain boasts some very distinguished holiday spots, namely the New Forest, the pleasant sandy beaches at Bournemouth, and the wonderful cathedral towns of Winchester and Salisbury, but it wasn't the easiest of areas to find a choice of vegetarian food.

The Town House in Southampton stands almost alone in this region as an example of how good vegetarian food can be and shows that it is possible to eat in some style. There are some other places to choose from that are strictly vegetarian, but these are more along the lines of simple cafés, with the standard of food ranging from reasonable to rather dull. Still, there are some non-vegetarian restaurants that cater quite well for vegetarians, and I was particularly impressed by a few of the pubs. An advantage of eating at a pub is that they tend to have food available on a Sunday when it can be difficult to get good food anywhere else.

The Bush Inn

Ovington, Nr Alresford, Hampshire
☎ 0962 732764
🏠 £5 bar, £12 restaurant

The village of Ovington consists of the Bush Inn and little else, but it's clearly a well-known, popular pub of the truly olde worlde, English country variety. I visited on a sunny day and enjoyed sitting in the rambling garden, where you can just hear the river Itchen gurgling by.

There are vegetarian choices in both the restaurant and at the bar.

The restaurant is more formal than the bar and the menu quite expensive. The starters are fairly ordinary — melon, avocado and so on. The main-course choices are a Pekinese stir-fry with fruit, nuts and rice, a ricotta tortellini and savoury crêpes with a mixed vegetable filling. The puddings are varieties of fruit served with varieties of alcohol! This would make a good place for dinner out, especially in a mixed party.

For those wanting a less formal meal, the bar menu is cheaper and less elaborate. The soup is home-made and will occasionally be suitable for vegetarians. The hot dish is a home-made mushroom and Stilton curry. On checking I was told that this was fine for vegetarians but not for vegans. It was quite tasty except for the gluey sauce and being a bit heavy on the mushrooms, but it came with brilliant yellow rice and a very spicy papadom. There were also some reasonable sandwiches. The vegetarian choice was amongst the other meaty menu items, which seems a good trend, as probably non-vegetarians will give them a try.

Open: 12-1.30, 7.30-9.30 Monday-Friday, 7.30-9.30 Saturday
(bar menu only on Sunday)
32 seats

The Cart and Horses Country Inn

Kings Worthy, Nr Winchester, Hampshire
☎ 0962 882360
🏠 £5

The Cart and Horses Country Inn is a lovely pub just a short way out of Winchester.

In the summer you can sit out in the garden or on the patio and enjoy a brilliant display of flowers. There are hanging baskets and tubs of geraniums and lobelia. Separating the garden from the patio is a majestic row of sunflowers. Inside it is a typical English country pub with a friendly atmosphere with a separate bar for ordering food.

The hot food suitable for vegetarians is a bit limited, but more than compensated for by the wonderful range of imaginative salads on offer. It is a 'help yourself' system and you can choose from eight salad mixtures, including a good coleslaw, creamy potato, beansprout, and Waldorf, as well as bowls full of tomato chunks, cucumber slices and beetroot. You could certainly make a meal of that, either with some chunky granary bread or a quiche, but check that the quiche is vegetarian. This has the advantage too of being a quick way to get your meal as the hot dishes do take some time to come.

I tried the tagliatelle, which was quite rich, very hot and fairly heavy on the cheese, but it too came with a decent salad garnish. There might also be a curry on offer.

The puddings are traditional, such as trifle, cheesecake and so on, and it is certainly worth checking on the ingredients. I tucked into the ripe blackberries in the nearby bushes, but these are not available all year round!

Open: 11.30-2, 6.30 onwards Monday-Saturday, til 7 Sunday
Credit cards: none
40 seats

     section

The Flying Teapot   ✓

25 Onslow Road, St Mary's, Southampton, Hampshire,
SO2 0JD
☎ 0703 335931
🏠 £3

Not at all formal, The Flying Teapot is run by a co-operative
and has variety of members serving who, when they are not
behind the counter, clearly enjoy a relaxing cigarette and a chat
at the central table!

There are notices galore advertising functions, concerts, clubs
and various agitprop. The place is popular with students and
quite affordable for them as the food is all extremely cheap.
Although I have given the average price above as £3, they do try
to make it possible to get a pretty basic meal for £1.

The counter is rather haphazard, things on the floor etc, but
you pays yer money as they say!

The menu — described very cleverly as the FT Index — covers
all the usual vegetarian things, in fact it would be more accurate
to say vegan as the only dairy product available is milk for tea
and coffee.

Hot savouries consisted of gigantic trays of vegetable bake and
the like and a few pasties, quiche and more snack-type items,
such as burgers, beans, tofu etc. I tried a vegetable pastie. The
filling tasted good, but the pastry was a bit dry. We also had a
take-away (10 per cent off!) portion of nut roast, which was
moist and tasty. I spied a delicious sorbet that someone else
ordered, clearly home-made.

I must say, I found the decaffeinated coffee was a bit grim —
you can bring your own wine though if you like (The Flying
Teapot is not licensed).

Do check that the place is still open if you are wanting to give
it a try — the collecting box on the counter in aid of the rent
arrears made me a little dubious about its future!

Open: 11-8.30 Monday-Saturday
Credit cards: none
32 seats

♿ 🍽 🚭 section

Henry's Wholefood Restaurant   √

6 Lansdowne Road, Bournemouth, Dorset, BH1 1SD
☎ 0202 297887
🏠💷 £7

This pleasant restaurant is in a small, terraced house quite close
to the town centre. The atmosphere is informal and the service
is efficient. On most days you can simply wander in for a meal,
but you may need to book on a Saturday evening.

The starters are good: lentil and walnut pâté, humus, crispy
cheese potato skins, and soup. There were four main courses
that were quite acceptable. We had vegetable moussaka and a
fruity butter bean curry. The portions are not huge, but a choice
of salad or vegetables and rice is included in the price so you
end up with a decent-sized meal.

There was a good selection of sweets, with a particularly good
boozy chocolate mousse, as well as chocolate and banana trifle,
and crumble. Again, the helpings were quite small.

Henry's is a good place to go for casual eating out rather than
as a venue for a special occasion.

Open: 11.30-2 Monday-Saturday, 11.30-2, 6-11 Tuesday-Friday
11.30-2, 6.30-11 Saturday
Credit cards: none
45 seats

 section

Inn-a-nutshell

The Dolphin Centre, Poole, Dorset, BH15 1SS
☎ 0202 673888
🏠 £3

This bright, modern café is a department of a larger restaurant called The Clipper (it also serves vegetarian food but is not exclusively vegetarian).

The food at Inn-a-nutshell is good value and there are some nice touches with unusual hot main courses such as oatmeal and cheese roast, mushroom delight, spinach Florentine, or African pilaff. The rest of the menu follows a predictable vegetarian format with soup, quiches, salads and so on. Most of the dishes are home-made and there is an emphasis on using fresh ingredients and wholemeal flour for baking.

A note for the disabled: there is access to this café and special toilet facilities just near by.

Open: 9.30-5 Monday-Saturday
Credit cards: none
65 seats
♿ 🚻 🍽 🚭

Minstrels

18 Little Minstrel Street, Winchester, Hampshire, SO23 9HB
☎ 0962 67212
🏠 £3

Tucked away down a little side street in the centre of Winchester
is Minstrels. It is quite a spacious café on the ground floor with
a large counter where you choose your food.

When we went, there were at least six salad mixtures on offer
with some imaginative combinations and a couple of tasty-
looking quiches. Sadly for us that day one was avocado and
prawn. However the other had a filling of three different-
coloured peppers, which was tasty, though the texture was less
than firm. The pizza slice was good. As for hot dishes, there
was a vegetable and cashew chilli, and a vegetable lasagne.
These are standard to the menu, but there is often a 'special'
that is also vegetarian and might be large, baked mushrooms,
stuffed courgettes or peppers.

The puddings are not generally wholefood. There could be
lemon meringue pie and, I was assured, a gelatine-free
cheesecake, but I think you should double-check. The cakes
looked more wholesome, though the biscuit I tried was very
sweet.

We were quite early and it wasn't too busy, which was lucky
as the service behind the counter seemed a little disorganized
and consequently rather slow.

In the summer of 1987, Minstrels opened a cellar restaurant in
the evening for the season, which also had vegetarian dishes as
a permanent feature on the menu. It is well worth checking to
see if they re-open this as, apart from a light lunch, it would
make a good place for a casual evening meal out.

Open: 9.30-5.30 Monday-Saturday
80 seats

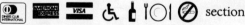 section

The Salad Centre

Post Office Road, Bournemouth, Dorset, BH1 1BA
☎ 0202 21720
🏠 £5

The Salad Centre is find for a lunch-time snack if you happen to
be in the vicinity.
   The decor is basic, as is the vegetarian menu. It consists of
jacket potatoes, pâté, humus, nut rissoles and, of course, salads.
They do cakes as well. The food we had tasted all right, but the
presentation was poor: the salads were all lumped together in a
small bowl and the hot dishes are microwaved in front of the
customer.

Open: 10.30-4.30 daily, with seasonal variations
Credit cards: none
60 seats
🍾 🍽 🚫 section

The Town House

59 Oxford Street, Southampton, Hampshire, SO1 1DL
☎ 0703 220498
🏠 £11.50 evening

The Town House is situated in the beautifully restored, award-winning area of old Southampton. Oxford Street is smart, and so too is this restaurant, with its elegant frontage and neat interior. There is a pleasing colour scheme with peach table cloths, which look good against the polished wood floor in the candlelight and fresh flowers adorn the tables.

Established some 14 years as a principally wholefood — including meat — restaurant, they began to offer a single vegetarian dish. As this gradually became more popular, three years ago they changed the place to make it all vegetarian and less wholefood, certainly on the pudding side.

Although they do open for morning coffee and light lunches — such as soup with bread, jacket potatoes, omelette and a dish of the day, such as lasagne or Chinese stuffed pancakes — their main trade is the gourmet evening meals.

In the evening, there is a set menu. You can choose from six starters, including soup, kiwi cocktail, dips with crudites, and six main courses. Some of the main-course dishes sound most exotic with epicure grilled avocado *au gratin*, asparagus *en croûte* or stuffed aubergine. All are well prepared and nicely presented. Some white rice is served and some things are made with white flour, and the same applies to the puddings. The menu always follows similar lines, but small changes are made throughout the year.

They take pride at The Town House in helping you make the most of your night out. It is certainly well patronized and so it is necessary to book at weekends. It is also small enough to be easily booked for a private party mid week to celebrate a special occasion.

Open: 12-2, 6.30-9 Tuesday-Friday, 12-2, 7-9 Saturday
        26 seats

West Country

Wiltshire, Avon, Devon, Cornwall, Somerset

This region of Britain is rich in places offering vegetarian food. What is special is that very many of them have an individual quality that adds greatly to the variety.

Many of the proprietors are 'amateurs' in that they love preparing and serving food, but have not necessarily had any formal training, so their approach to the business is often imaginative and instinctive. The cafés and restaurants are, therefore, run on quite a small scale, which means the owner is not only head chef but chief bottle washer as well. In my experience as a restaurateur, such closeness to any operation seems a recipe for success.

There is really excellent day-time food to be had in both the relatively unsophisticated restaurants, such as Stones, which is my personal favourite in this part of England, or McCreadies, as well as delicious, more up-market evening eating at Willow and Millwards.

Throughout the rest of the region, there are reliable wholefood establishments and some interesting non-vegetarian restaurants, such as Loaves and Fishes, Bakers or Toppers, where you can get good evening meals in pleasant surroundings. It is a little disappointing to find, however, that places get a little thin on the ground the closer you get to the toe of England.

Acorn

40 Havelock Street, Swindon, Wiltshire, SN1 1SD
☎ 0793 39396
🏠 £5 day; £11 evening

Acorn has developed from a small, wholefood café and shop into a fully fledged restaurant. The shop has gone and, in its place, there is a wine bar area, serving casual snacks and take-aways, and a restaurant upstairs with table service. Acorn is open all day and, in the evening, there are extra comforts, such as table linen, candlelight and sweet music.

The take-away service includes a wide range of sandwiches, quiches, pasties and salads, as well as frozen meals, bread and cakes.

The restaurant menu here now includes seafood during the day and some meat is served in the evenings, but there is still a good and varied selection for vegetarians with a wholefood emphasis. Starters include home-made soup, melon cocktail and mushrooms in a creamy sauce.

There are stuffed pancakes, bean bakes and a fair range of side-salads, as well as more interesting dishes, such as Moroccan stuffed vegetables with a *compote* of sweetened tomatoes and almonds, or fricassee of exotic vegetables in a light flaky pastry. There are good, home-made puds as well, plus Loseley ice-creams and sorbets.

Open: 9am-10.30pm Monday-Saturday
80 seats

 section

Bakers of Ninetree Hill

3 Ninetree Hill, Stokes Croft, Bristol, Avon, BS1 3SB
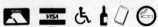 0272 47242
£8

I would highly recommend this restaurant with its small but
thoughtful menu and pleasant atmosphere. You can eat in either
the Edwardian-style dining room or one of the two more
intimate cellar rooms. The bigger of these is an ideal place to
celebrate for a party.

There is a set three-course menu, which changes every four
weeks. The starters are mainly vegetarian, light and imaginative,
such as walnut and spring onion tarts, mushrooms with a garlic
and honey dressing, and carrot and lemon soup.

There are two main courses, which could have been inspired
by a number of different cuisines. When we visited there was
broccoli and walnut croustade or vine leaves stuffed with a
traditional pine kernel and rice mixture, mildly spiced. Menus
have also featured mushroom and lentil *gratin*, and hazelnut and
courgette loaf with a sweet-and-sour sauce. These are served
with hot seasonal vegetables and, sometimes, a salad.

The home-made ice-creams are a speciality here. All sorts of
lovely combinations are possible: apricot and almond, avocado
and honey, and the ever-popular brown bread. There is always
something of the more rib-sticking variety if you wish, such as
plum and cinnamon crumble, or sticky toffee pudding.

Although the restaurant is entirely smoking, because there are
a choice of rooms you can always mention that you would
prefer a non-smoking area.

Open: 7-10.30 Tuesday-Thursday, 7-11 Friday and Saturday
35 seats

Cranks

Shinners Bridge, Dartington, Nr Totnes, Devon, TQ9 6JB
 0803 862388
£4

I have always wanted to visit the West Country offshoot of the famous London Cranks, and now I know why. The first impressions make you feel that it is going to be exactly the same, as the decor follows the London Cranks style of plain wooden tables and benches, cane lampshades and beautifully scripted notices thanking you for returning your tray and so on. The buffet counter too is loaded with all the same sorts of cheese baps, massive bowls of salads, sweets and savouries, but there is something different about the food here. The presentation seems better. The salads are more attractive and interesting and the toppings and fillings for the pizzas and pies are more generous. Part of the reason for this, perhaps, is that they are producing smaller quantities and there is still room for some spontaneous variation and an individual touch.

The restaurant is part of a large craft and shop complex. There are some good bargains to be had in the glass and pottery sections, as well as a wide choice of gifts and handmade items. It does get very busy in summer and is part of the itinerary of some coach tours, so you need to time your visit well.

Open: 9.30-5 daily (closed Sundays in winter)
Credit cards: none
80 seats plus garden and patio

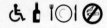

The Goat House

Bristol Road, Brent Knoll, Somerset TA9 4HJ
☎ 0278 760650
🏠 £3

Brent Knoll is a landmark, rising out of the Somerset wetlands, and there is a marvellous panorama if you have the energy to climb to its summit.

There is plenty to see here apart from the view as The Goat House is one of a group of buildings set up to develop and promote the wide range of products from goats. Marjorie and Tony Jarvis, the owners, started with just 12 animals — they now have 200. They assure you that the animals are friendly, inquisitive and enjoy being visited, but they might just run off with your lunch if you let them!

The chef is vegetarian and produces a small vegetarian menu of snacks and light meals. Obviously relies quite heavily on dairy products, including cheese baked potatoes, ploughman's platters and pizza. There are salads as well and these are very fresh, made to order and include quite a good range of ingredients.

Good home-made wholemeal cakes are also on sale, plus herbal teas and freshly brewed coffee.

Open: 9-5.30 Monday, 12-5.30 Tuesday, 9-5.30 Wednesday-
      Sunday
Credit cards: none
50 seats
🍽️ 🚭 section

The Good Earth

4 Priory Road, Wells, Somerset BA5 1SY
☎ 0749 78600
🏠 £3 day; £10 evening

Serving decent home-made food at very reasonable prices, The
Good Earth is typical of so many vegetarian wholefood places.
Start with a bowl of soup and follow with snacks, such as pizza
and baked potato with a choice of fillings, or a hot main course,
such as nut and mushroom loaf or lasagne. Great bowls of
salads and a tempting array of cheesecakes, gâteaux and plenty
of desserts using fresh fruit complete the lunch-time choice.

They also do a take-away service, as I discovered when I
arrived with a hamperless party wanting to go on a picnic. We
were instantly accommodated with a couple of very tasty
quiches. The staff are very friendly and genuinely helpful,
especially with children, offering feeder cups and high chairs.
There's even a place for changing the baby!

Established nearly ten years as a good place to get wholesome
daily fare, The Good Earth is trying now to make a success of
openings in the evenings as well. The simple day-time decor is
enriched in the evenings with red linen napkins, candles and
floral arrangements. The menu changes too, offering more
elaborate concoctions. The style of service changes as well, with
the food being brought to your table so you have more of a
chance to relax and enjoy your meal. They have a range of
special wines, non-alcoholic beers and other soft drinks.

Open: 9.30-5.30 Monday and Tuesday, 9.30-5.30, 7-10
      Wednesday-Saturday
80 seats

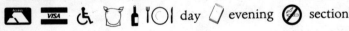 day   evening   section

The Greenhouse   ✓

Madford Lane, Launceston, Cornwall PL15 9AB
 0566 3670
£4

The Greenhouse lives up to its name with its refreshing decor of green and white furniture and plenty of plants. French café lighting adds a sophisticated touch, and the overall effect is clean and spacious. There is a tasteful, modern counter where you go to choose your food.

The menu is quite straightforward. Every day there is a choice of soup, pizza slices, quiche and either nut or bean burgers, served with salad or jacket potato. I had the bean burgers, which were tasty and filling. The pizza had a soft base and substantial filling.

The main courses change daily and it could feature ratatouille lasagne, green bean and mushroom bake or lentils *au gratin*. These also come served with salads. There are about six types of salad, which will vary according to the season. Apart from the predictable coleslaw and greenery, I had a rather unusual cooked carrot and spring onion.

They seldom make puddings here, but occasionally you can have apple pie with clotted cream. However, they do have a lovely range of cakes and slices, banana and nut, date flapjack, chocolate or coffee cake. All the usual drinks are also available.

The cooking here is done with care and you feel that the watchful eye of the owners make sure everything is just right. They have a nice manner with the regulars too, discussing diets with one couple, and welcoming someone else with 'we've got your favourite on today'. The smiling service makes for a homely atmosphere — no wonder they feel able to open on Christmas Day! The only thing I found a little twee was the soft background music.

Open: 9-4 Monday-Saturday*
Credit cards: none
46 seats

🍷 🍽 ⃠

* Closed Thursdays from October to March.

The Health Food Store, Natural Choice ✓

84 Lemon Street, Truro, Cornwall TR1 2QA
☎ 0872 75344
🎒 £4

Opened in 1988, this simple, first-floor café has a fresh, modern feeling. Everything on the menu is either home-made or produced locally and, although the menu is small, there is certainly plenty to satisfy the appetite.

There are all types of snack items, such as pasties, samosas, quiche and jacket potatoes with various fillings. These come with an ample bowlful of salad, brimming with different ingredients and served with a separate container of French dressing.

For the hungrier amongst you, there are two 'Hot specials', such as lasagne, curry, bean casserole or shepherd's pie to choose from.

To complete your meal, there are all the usual wholefood cakes and slices as well as ice-cream that can be had from the shop downstairs.

This is a pleasant place for a good-value meal.

Open: 10-4 Monday-Saturday
Credit cards: none
26 seats

Honeybees

110 High Street, Honiton, Devon EX14 8JW
☎ 0404 43392
 £4

This restaurant, on Honiton's main street, was started up some four years ago, and the emphasis is on wholefood rather than vegetarian, though very little meat is cooked. They try to buy as much local produce as possible, including free-range eggs.

The restaurant is quite small and looks very cosy with Laura Ashley-style wallpaper panels and table-cloths and homely displays of knick-knackery.

The menu is quite simple. There is always a vegetable curry and then one other hot choice, such as red dragon pie, stir-fry vegetables or lasagne. These change frequently according to what is in season. There is always a vegetarian soup, and lighter meals of quiche, jacket potato, and baked beans.

Cakes, such as carrot cake and passion cake, are made locally and, apart from these wholesome varieties, the odd sticky one is on sale, too.

Honeybees is certain a good watering-hole if you are on the long journey down to the West Country.

Open: 9-5 Monday-Saturday (5.30 summer)
Credit cards: none
36 seats
♿ ◻ 🚭 section

Huckleberry's

34 Broad Street, Bath, Avon, BA1 5LP
☎ 0225 64876
📖 £4 day, £10 evening

Strangers to Bath may find Huckleberry's hard to spot. We
drove around several times, entirely missing the little sign, so be
prepared to look carefully.

Huckleberry's is an informal restaurant with simple seating
and plenty of plants to liven up the decor. Here you can get a
good-value, wholesome lunch, but in the evening they really try
to make you feel you are having a special night out. 'Posher'
was the owner's word for it, but, in fact, it means table service,
sultry lighting, candles, a more gourmet menu — and it works!

The restaurant is split-level and you can see into the busy,
small kitchen where you go to order food during the day. There
are all the usual dishes — quiche, bakes and casseroles, with a
choice of salads and the menu changes daily.

The evening menu is entirely different and draws on a range of
international ideas. Each dish has a few imaginative touches in
terms of garnish or accompaniment, which make such a
difference. Pinto bean casserole is served with corn bread and
sour cream, buckwheat crêpes, stuffed with aubergine and
mushrooms, are smothered in a red wine sauce, or there's gado
gado, a spicy peanut sauce, served over barely-cooked
vegetables and brown rice. It is all prepared well and looks
appetizing on the plate. The service is very friendly and efficient
but not at all intrusive.

Huckleberry's has been going seven years or so, but it's
certainly not stale. They seem to be aware of changing
requirements — like the fact that vegetarians do enjoy having a
stylish night out. It is certainly worth a visit.

Open: 10-10 Monday-Saturday
60 seats

▨ ≟ ⵏ◎⎸ day ▱ evening ⊘ section

Jenner's Wholefood Café

45 Market Place, Warminster, Wiltshire, BA12 9AZ
☎ 0985 213385
 £5

This simple café consists of a rather plain, square room with a small counter at the back and a tiny area where you can buy wholefoods. The stripped pine tables are well spaced, and you can order from the printed menu or the daily specials chalked up on the board.

The service is very friendly and obliging — the staff were very helpful when we tried to order various combinations of items that weren't on the menu! The food listed is all appetizingly described, but I found my half-filled bowl of rather indifferent watercress soup somewhat disappointing after the glowing billing it had been given (thick, heartwarming and so on). The bread and butter with it though were fine, and things certainly picked up with the main course, which was a very tasty cheese quiche that I felt lived up to its description on the menu. The side-salad was uninspiring.

Both the coffee and cakes were good, and the hot, spicy apple juice was terrific.

Jenner's is open at the weekends just before Christmas and offers a special menu. Do ring for details.

Open: 9.30-5.30 daily (closed Sunday October-Easter)
Credit cards: none
48 seats

Loaves and Fishes

Rockley, Nr Marlborough, Wiltshire, SN8 1RT
☎ 0672 53737
£17

Loaves and Fishes is an unusual, small restaurant set in a converted chapel in a little village on the Broad Hinton road between Swindon and Marlborough. It has built up a very good following locally.

The service here is very personal, classical music plays in the background and wall hangings are used to divide the space into cosy areas.

Although it is expensive, it is certainly worth visiting for special occasions. It is essential to book and also to tell them that you would like the vegetarian menu.

We had two delicious starters of pear with Stilton sauce, and a very good avocado and walnut purée with warm, home-made rolls. The main course was a chestnut and mushroom casserole with a 'duvet' of pastry, served with perfectly cooked vegetables.

For dessert there were several choices, from the rich, chocolate and banana mousse to simple fresh fruit, that was excellently presented. There was also a cheese board with crackers, though you should check the fat content, and tangy rye bread.

Although they are not licensed, you are very welcome to bring your own wine to have with your meal if you wish.

Overall it was an excellent meal, worth the money, and definitely worth finding an excuse to go again.

Open: 7.30-11 Wednesday-Saturday, lunch from 12.30 Sunday
25 seats

McCreadies

26 Broad Street, Bristol, Avon, BS1 2HG
☎ 0272 265580
🏠 £4

This restaurant is conveniently situated right in the heart of
Bristol's city centre, hence their long weekday opening hours so
people can have a decent breakfast before a day's work.

Even if you are a visitor, rather than a local, it is definitely
worth visiting McCreadies. It is in an interesting location,
opposite the Everard building, a unique Art Nouveau-tiled
edifice, and nearby is St John's Gate, the only piece of the
original city wall still standing.

Apart from sightseeing, the food is great and excellent value.
As much as 80 per cent of the vegetables they use are organic
and nearly 100 per cent of the fruit. Everything here is
home-made.

You can choose from soup and bread with spread, plus several
'Hot specials' — at least one of which will be vegan. We had
spinach and cheese croquettes, which were very tasty. Chick pea
cobbler is a favourite, and ratatouille bake. The main courses
come with salads, and there are usually half a dozen to choose
from. They come with interesting dressings and pleasant, fresh
flavours. One slight problem is that the food is microwaved as
you wait for it and, inevitably, this slows the whole process
down, making queues rather lengthy.

McCreadies began opening in the evenings not so long ago,
limiting it to two nights a week. You'll get the same good value
with a set meal at £10, including wine!

Highly recommended.

Open: 8.30-5 Monday-Wednesday, 8.30-5, 7.30-12 Thursday
and Friday, 11-5 Saturday winter; 8.30-9 Monday-
Wednesday, 8.30-5, 7.30-12 Thursday and Friday, 11-5
Saturday summer
Credit cards: none
40 seats

🍷 🍽 📖 🚭 section

Mainly Salads

18 Fisherton Street, Salisbury, Wiltshire, SP6 3BQ
☎ 0722 22134
 £3

There is an appropriately green feel to Mainly Salads, a spacious city-centre restaurant suitable for wholesome, day-time eating.

The menu changes daily with everything chalked up on a small blackboard, and, indeed, while we had our lunch, fresh dishes were constantly being brought out of the kitchen. The food is on display on a large counter as you go in. The main courses are kept warm on a hotplate.

I chose an open vegetable pie with a crunchy crumble topping. The filling was great, but the pastry was somewhat reminiscent of cardboard. We also had a slice of nut roast which had good texture and a surprising kick of chilli. The salads were varied with nice mixtures of ingredients; coleslaw with apple and grapes, rice with green lentils, spring onions and mushrooms, for example. The dressings, however, were rather limited — mayonnaise or nothing. The portions, though, were huge and very good value at under 50p each.

For pudding there was apple pie, apricot cream and a cheesecake, which, I was told, contained gelatine (so watch out any unsuspecting vegetarians).

Nice though this place was, it describes itself as vegetarian, and you would therefore expect all the food to be suitable for vegetarians.

Open: 10-5 Monday-Saturday (annual hols 1 week in Sept)
Credit cards: none
50 seats

⅃ 🍴 🚭

Millwards

40 Alfred Place, Kingsdown, Bristol, Avon, BS2 8HD
 0272 245026
£9

This pleasant candlelit restaurant can be found in a quiet
Regency backwater in Bristol. The atmosphere is relaxed,
intimate and quite informal.

John and Pat Millward have tried to leave the stripped pine
image of vegetarianism very far behind. The tables have simple
white cloths, silver cutlery and plain pink and terracotta walls.
They have chosen to have an open-plan kitchen so that the
process of preparing and cooking food is a feature of the
restaurant.

There is a menu with about four or five main-course choices
that changes every couple of months. Two more main courses
and extra starters are chalked up on the blackboard and these
vary during the week. They try to have a couple of starters and
main courses that are suitable for vegans.

The food here is light and stylish with a nice range of
ingredients used and unusual combinations. To begin your meal
you could have caribbean pâté with oat biscuits, spinach, cheese
and pine kernels in filo pastry with soured cream, or avocado
dip with crudites. Main courses include a vegan mediterranean
pasta, cashew and mushroom roast with red wine sauce, leek,
cheese and almond turnover with spiced yoghurt, or mushroom
gougère. All these come with either hot vegetables or salad,
which is served separately. The portions are generous, and the
food is nicely presented with lots of fresh herbs used for
garnish.

Puddings are rich and sweet. The brown sugar meringues are
very popular, served with cream and ice-cream, or there is
chocolate and hazelnut slice with chocolate chip ice-cream.
Vegan puddings include fresh date and apple mousse or terrine
of sorbets with apricot sauce.

Millwards is a delightful place that is ideal for casual *and*
special occasions and is well worth a visit.

Open: 7-10.30 Tuesday-Saturday
27 seats

The Old Bakehouse

High Street, Castle Cary, Somerset BA7 7AW
☎ 0963 50067
🏠 £4

Even in winter you may need to book a table at this very
popular little restaurant. We were lucky enough to get the last
unreserved table at midday.

The menu is quite straightforward and relies heavily on dairy
products. Main courses consist of quiche, pizza, pepper
croustade, and egg mayonnaise with salad.

The main appeal of the place is the homeliness of the cooking.
We tried the pizza, which was piping hot and tasty with a rather
doughy base, served with a lovely side-salad, all presented on
an attractive oval plate. The salad consisted of chunks of fresh
fruit, a nice mixture of vegetables and a spoonful of moist rice.

The coffee was excellent, as was the delicious apple and
coconut cake and the service was quick and friendly.

Lunches only are served between midday and 2 o'clock and
during the rest of the day you can sample other home-made
cakes and scones.

In the summer it is possible to sit out in the attractive
courtyard at the back of the restaurant.

Open: 9-5.30 Tuesday-Saturday
Credit cards: none
28 seats
♿ 🍼 📋 🚭

The Polly Tea Rooms

High Street, Marlborough, Wiltshire SN8 1LW
☎ 0672 52146
☕ £5

This is a pretty, olde worlde tea room on Marlborough's High
Street. It is very well known for its cakes, biscuits, gâteaux and
traditional lunch but they do offer some vegetarian fare.

There is a choice of a hot main course or a plate of mixed
salad. The choice is a little limited, but what there is good and
this alone makes The Polly worthy of inclusion here, even more
so because the number of vegetarian eating places in this part of
the world are a little thin on the ground.

The hot savoury dish the day we visited was a delicious
broccoli crêpe, which was tasty and piping hot. The choice may
sometimes be rather more mundane, such as quiche. A regular
feature of the menu, though, is the salad platter. It was a very
fresh and imaginative mixture that any fully fledged vegetarian
place would be proud to serve. There were several different sorts
of salad, such as pasta, celery and nut, carrot and coleslaw, all
arranged in spoonfuls on the plate with a standard lettuce
garnish.

The service is friendly and efficient and the restaurant cosy
and comfortably furnished. Beware the wickedly tempting range
of chocolates on sale on the way out, though!

Open: 8.30-6 Monday-Friday, 8-7 Saturday, 9-7 Sunday
110 seats

      section

Rainbow's End Cafe

17a High Street, Glastonbury, Somerset, BA6 9DP
☎ 0458 33896
🏠 £3

Rainbow's End started life as a greasy spoon, had a phase as a hippy place and is now firmly established as a good-value café, serving a range of simple, wholesome dishes that appeal to a wide range of folk. There's a friendly feel about the place with lively staff, a hotpotch mixture of tables, and walls adorned with local pictures.

It is amazing that they can produce so much good food from the tiny kitchen, but plans are afoot to increase the space. The food is served on chunky pottery and the portions are generous.

There is always a vegan soup and a choice of main-course bakes and casseroles, as well as all the usual snack items, such as pizzas, quiches, jacket potatoes and so on. The menu changes daily, depending on the fancy of the chef as much as on what is available.

Having been good and healthy for the first two courses, you can indulge in a suitably wicked, gooey pudding, which seems to be a speciality, as well as a lovely range of cakes and slices.

During the height of the summer season, this place becomes exceedingly crowded, so, either try to go at less busy times of the year or be prepared for a short but worthwhile wait (there are some tables outside at the back to cope with any overspill).

Open: 10-4.30 Monday and Tuesday, Thursday-Saturday
Credit cards: none
50 seats

 ♿ 🍼 🍽 🚭

Reapers

23 Gold Street, Tiverton, Devon, EX16 6QD
☎ 0884 255310
🏠 £2

The small café here has really grown out of the wholefood shop, and the proprietors have found that, despite the limitations of size, it is proving extremely popular with plenty of local support.

There is usually a dish of the day — along simple lines of hot-pot, ratatouille, lasagne or vegetable bake — all at the amazing price of around £1 — as well as soup, quiche and baked potato. There are some salads as well, and the mixture depends very much on what happens to be available.

There are sometimes cakes and slices but usually only on the busier days.

The café itself is clean, pleasant and ideal for a cheap vegetarian lunch, whether you are just in town shopping or on holiday in the area.

Open: 10-3 Monday-Saturday
Credit cards: none
20 seats

Stones

High Street, Avebury, Wiltshire, SN8 1RF
☎ 06723 514
£5

Avebury is a delightful place. The village is almost part of the unique circle of standing stones. These are not as large as the ones at Stonehenge, but they are more accessible. You can walk in amongst the stones and around the whole circle. Silbury Hill — an enormous man-made mound — and the ancient Ridgeway are close by.

I've driven 50 miles out of my way in the past *just* to have food at Stones — it is *that* good! It is near The National Trust Shop and Wiltshire Archaeological Museum, housed in a large barn.

As you enter you see a marvellous display of salads, savouries and cakes. The friendly and very knowledgeable staff help you choose (if you can bear not to try everything!) and explain any of the dishes. You can sit either at the simple tables inside, or have unlimited space out of doors when it is warm.

The food here is truly first class, imaginative and tasty. As seasonal ingredients are used wherever possible, there are different combinations daily although the basic structure of the menu remains the same. For lunch, there are two soups — perhaps courgette and mushroom with dill picked in the garden or parsnip and orange — six different quiches, including one made with organic spinach, and a French bean *provençale*. They also make six 'Hot specials'. The majority of these are their own inventions and there are some wonderfully imaginative dishes. You may be offered Papadzules loaf — of Mexican origin with fresh salsa and soured cream — or aubergine korma with summer fruit curry and wild rice. There are salads too, constantly changing through the day so if you sit there long enough you might see at least 15 concoctions!

There is a staggering variety of food produced here with different ideas on offer each day.

If you only want afternoon tea, it's tremendous for that, too. The counter is overloaded with a splendid array of cakes and slices, Bakewell tart, carob cakes, apple cakes, shortbread, scones — the list is endless.

Stones is marvellous place to eat. It is unpretentious, concerned with quality and, above all, it probably does not occur to the majority of diners that it is vegetarian. One thing is sure — I'd defy them to *miss* meat!

Open: 10-6 daily from Easter to end October[*]
200 seats

♿ 🍽 🛏 ⊘ section

Toppers

40 Fore Street, Topsham, nr. Exeter, Devon, EX3 0HU
☎ 0392 874707
 £10

Blackboards abound at this intimate, bistro-style restaurant at the top end of Topsham's narrow high street. It is certainly worth driving here from Exeter and beyond to sample the satisfying vegetarian food. The menu is predominantly vegetarian with some fish and one meat dish on offer.

There are some rich starters, such as Stilton and port pâté, as well as fresh fruit ideas such as plain melon or pineapple with a herb and yoghurt dressing. The main courses have their roots in a variety of cuisines and have a wholefood emphasis. There is a robust cashew and mushroom bake, wholewheat spaghetti and mushroom *provençale*, and a lighter spinach and celery roulade. The menu changes every so often according to what vegetables are available and whether a new dish turns out to be popular.

Sunday lunch is excellent value at £5.15 with a choice for vegetarians of soup, humus or vegetable pâté for starters, and a main course of cauliflower and almond roast or courgette and lentil pie.

Puddings consist of a variety of ice-creams, with hot and cold sweets that are along the usual lines (profiteroles, hot chocolate fudge cake, and so on), with the exception of one item — they have a suet-free Christmas pudding on the menu, all year round!

Open: 6.30-10 Monday-Saturday, 12.30-2, 6.30-9.30 Sunday
24 seats

Trugs

5 Union Street, Yeovil, BA20 1PQ
☎ 0935 73722
£4

Trugs is a wholefood restaurant where the emphasis is on using fresh foods and trying to avoid chemicals, colourings and soon wherever possible. All the items, except the bread and ice-cream, are made on the premises.

We tried both the soups — a good carrot and coriander and a slightly watery leek and potato. The main courses are chalked up on the blackboard and change daily. When we went there was mushroom risotto, courgette *provençale* on brown rice and vegetable moussaka. Plenty of snack-type meals are available: pitta bread filled with cottage cheese, or mushrooms in yoghurt, a ploughman's and mixed or plain salads. They do quiches too, which come in very generous portions. The broccoli one I tried was quite tasty.

There were standard puddings on offer, such as apple crumble and some good-looking cakes. The staff are friendly, and the food is presented on pleasing pottery.

Trugs is quite large, furnished with modern wooden tables, and there is a smoking area down a few steps. We had lunch mid afternoon so it wasn't crowded and I had the feeling that, while it was all pleasant enough, everything was a little tired at the edges. They have closed their branch in Southampton, so I hope they continue in Yeovil. Perhaps extra business will give the owners new heart.

Open: 9.30-5 Monday-Saturday
Credit cards: none
64 seats
🍷 ▱ 🚭 section

Willow   ✓

87 High Street, Totnes, Devon TQ9 5PB
☎ 0803 862605
🏠 £4 day, £7 evening

Willow is the flagship of an enthusiastic colony of wholefooders
in Totnes. It is to be found at the top end of the quaint high
street. The decor is sparse with uncovered wooden tables, bold
bunches of fresh flowers and the walls adorned with African
photographs. There are collecting jars on the counter in aid of
tropical rain forests and other ecological causes.

The restaurant is open for day and evening meals and the
menu remains more or less the same. In the day the food tends
to be a little more basic, with starters such as soup, main
courses of quiche, pizza and a vegan dish, served with or
without salad as you choose, jacket potatoes and a range of
cakes and crumbles. They note on the menu that the sweet
things are usually sweetened with honey or sugar substitutes.

At night the food tends to be more exotic. The night I went,
the soup was flageolet with juniper berries and came in very
generous portions. We also tried the tofu and herb dip. It came
with a fresh salad garnish and hot pitta bread. The texture of
the dip was light and extremely creamy.

The main courses at night are automatically served with salad.
Everything gets put on one plate, making it hard to distinguish
the different types. I do feel this rather lets down the
presentation but, niceties apart, it tasted excellent. There was a
tasty mushy bean salad, and a good mixture of red cabbage and
hazelnut, mixed in with some powerfully flavoured leaves. For
my main course I had the broccoli and lemon bake. The texture
was pleasantly creamy, offset by the tangy breadcrumb topping.
The tagliatelle with creamy mushroom sauce was good.

Still room for pudding? It was hard to choose between
Granny's buckwheat and cranberry cake and the carob mousse.
The million calories a mouthful mousse won! I made the most
of every morsel and was glad to finish with lemon verbena tea.

There is also table service in the evenings, and you are served
remarkably quickly. The overall atmosphere is low key. I envy
the locals of Totnes for having this place on their doorstep.
Certainly it would influence any choice of route I make in the
West Country in the future.

Open: 9-5, 6.30-10 Monday-Saturday July-September, 10-5
     Monday and Tuesday, 10-5, 6.30-10 Wednesday, 10-5
     Thursday, 10-5, 6.30-10 Friday and Saturday
     October-June
Credit cards: none
55 seats plus

  ♿ 🍾 🍽 day 🔥 evening 🚭

The Wiltshire Kitchen

St John's Street, Devizes, Wiltshire, SN10 1BD
☎ 0380 4840
🏠 £5

A bustling servery and a distinctively WI feel greet you at the Wiltshire Kitchen.

They certainly know how to bake to a high standard and your best bet, as a vegetarian, is to go for a classic dish, such as quiche. My cheese and spinach one was very tasty. Other food on offer is passable, but you do feel they are making an effort for vegetarians. The stuffed cannelloni, though, was rather bland. There looked to be a good range of salad mixtures, to which you help yourself, but, on closer inspection, they were all rather dull: a pile of plain red kidney beans, unflavoured bulgar wheat, a bit of mixed greenery, and coleslaw. At least you can pick out the best with the help-yourself system. As an alternative they do offer a selection of hot vegetables.

The puddings run along traditional lines and there are plenty of good home-made cakes.

Open: 9.30-5.30 Monday-Saturday
Credit cards: none
60 seats

🍷 🍽 📄 🚭

The Thames and Chilterns

Bedfordshire, Buckinghamshire, Hertfordshire, Oxfordshire, Berkshire

Few of the places reviewed in this area are wholly vegetarian, but there is some decent food on offer and a nice mixture of venues — from the rather eccentric Cook's Delight in Berkhamsted to the smart, stylish restaurants in Woodstock and Potton. Oxford, being one of the most popular tourist traps, has quite a selection of eating places, though, again, nothing completely vegetarian.

More into the heart of the Cotswolds there are one or two places that I've discovered where you can eat very well.

Much of this region now is, to a certain extent, London overflow, though I'm sure this description will infuriate many locals. It is the case, though, that many who live around the Thames and Chilterns spend a great deal of their time on busy commuter trains and even more crowded motorways to the capital. Considering the density of the population in the areas to the north and west of London it is disappointing that there are so few vegetarian restaurants.

Brothertons Brasserie

1 High Street, Woodstock, Oxfordshire, OX4 1TE
☎ 0993 811114
£6

Brothertons is an attractive looking restaurant with a French feel
to the interior — and to the quality of the coffee, which is
excellent! The decor is dark wood, with small, round tables on
wrought-iron bases, and gas lighting, supplied by a tiny exposed
pipe that runs at picture-rail height around the walls.

There is always one choice for a vegetarian — a *plat du jour*,
which will vary according to the season and what is available at
the market. Stuffed courgettes or peppers, mushroom Stroganoff
or vegetable pancakes might be on offer. For starters there are a
few more choices, though they are rather predictable — melon,
avocado or deep-fried mushrooms.

Desserts include a rich chocolate mousse, but also Greek
yoghurt and honey, as well as more traditional puds, such as
rhubarb crumble.

The cooking is of a high standard, and Brothertons, even
though it has a casual atmosphere, is fairly sophisticated. In this
area, where there is a dearth of suitable eating places, it is a
useful venue and somewhere to go with a mixed party.

Open: 12-2.30, 6.30-10.30 daily
65 seats

Café MOMA

30 Pembroke Street, Oxford, OX1 1BP
☎ 0865 722733
🏠 £4

Situated in the heart of Oxford, below the Museum of Modern
Art, Café MOMA specializes in wholefood cuisine and, though
not all the menu is vegetarian, the manager has a preference for
non-meat dishes.

The café is in a large, basement room, with a pleasantly light
atmosphere, thanks to the modern tables, bright green chairs
and good lighting — no smoking. Everything is very reasonable
priced.

The soup used to be made from fresh chicken stock until so
many people wanted a meat-free version that they decided to
cater to the demand. It is always quite hearty, and you can have
some of the lovely range of breads with it, rye or wholemeal.
The breads are virtually the only items not made on the
premises.

There are some substantial main courses, such as vegetable
chilli, mushroom and courgette loaf or cheese and walnut loaf,
both of which can be served hot or cold and come with salads.
There are also more snack-type foods such as filo pastry, filled
with spinach, cheese and currants, and quiche.

You'll find several salads to choose from, both lightweight,
French-style, mainly greenery, and robust lentil mixtures.

What I liked at Café MOMA was the willingness of the staff to
explain about ingredients and help with any dietary requests.
You can be sure they know the ingredients of anything on offer.
As yet vegan dishes are not regularly on the menu.

On Sundays there is only afternoon tea, but I wouldn't mind
having their delicious chocolate Rembrandt cake.

Open: 10-5 Tuesday-Saturday, 2-5 Sunday
Credit cards: none
70 seats

 ♿ 🍴 🍽 🚭

Cook's Delight

360-364 High Street, Berkhamsted, Hertfordshire HP4 1HU
☎ 0442 863584
🏠 £17

Highly recommended for an eccentric night out. You will be entertained by Rex Tyler, a terrific food buff (not food bore), who gives you nutritional tips as he serves the meal, and these slip down as easily as the excellent food!

The atmosphere is very warm with an oriental flavour — there are cushions scattered around and music to meditate to. On Saturday nights, there are a variety of special evenings, such as 'South East Asian Seafood Special', 'Malaysian Cookery', or 'South East Asian Vegetarian Gourmet', which is the one we tried.

On these nights everyone is served the same food together, and it feels like a special party. You can bring your own wine too to add to the atmosphere! It is a four-course meal, featuring a most exotic range of ingredients. We had stir-fried pak choi and tofu, followed by lime leaf tempeh curry. Then we had a mushroom and leek dish with rice sticks and finally gado gado — a spicy sauce, served with melon, aubergine and pineapple. All these are eaten out of the same bowl, with chop sticks (optional).

The meal is certainly a different type of experience, good if you are on a vegan or strict macrobiotic diet, and interesting if you are not, plus the added bonus of sharing Rex's vast nutritional knowledge.

There are traditional puddings to follow, such as apple pie, lemon meringue and ice-cream. These cost £2 extra.

Cook's Delight print a list of their special evenings, though occasionally these are subject to change. It is essential that you book in advance as they are very popular.

At lunch-times, you serve yourself and, on Thursday and Friday, you can have an 'eat-as much-as-you-like' platter for £5.50.

Open: 12-2 Thursday-Sunday, 8pm Saturday South East Asian
      cuisine
42 seats

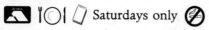 Saturdays only

Go Dutch

18 Park End Street, Oxford OX1 18U
☎ 0865 240686
🏠 £5

This traditional Dutch pancake house is practically the first
building that greets you as you leave Oxford station. Smartly
painted on the outside, it has a charming interior. The walls are
partly covered with classic Dutch blue and white tiles and a
wonderful selection of bric-a-brac. There are giant cheese plants,
old pitchers and wash bowls, and beautiful, painted glass
lampshades, hung low over each table. Newspapers are available
for you to browse through while you enjoy your meal.

Hartige pannekoeken — country-style Dutch pancakes, made
from a very light, wholemeal batter — are the main feature of
the savoury menu. There was a special of the day — a filling of
walnut, apple and celery — and then a choice of other set
fillings. Most of these contain meat, but there is a list of
individual fillings, such as pineapple, apple, sweetcorn, peppers,
mushrooms, etc., that you can order singly or in combination
with a plain pancake.

These pancakes are cooked and served in an entirely different
way to English ones. Whatever you choose for your filling —
mushrooms, peppers or whatever — is cooked first and then the
batter is poured over the top. The finished pancake is served flat
on a plate, topped with butter. There's a sprinkling of fresh
herbs if what you have chosen needs more flavouring. There's
also a side-salad.

Sweet pancakes or Dutch apple pie are available if you still
have some space left.

Open: 12-2.30, 6-11 Monday-Friday, 12-11 Saturday and
        Sunday
Credit cards: none
40 seats

Nutters

10 New Street, Chipping Norton, Oxfordshire; OX7 5LJ
☎ 0608 41995
🏠 £4

Nutters is a charming little restaurant just round the corner from
the main shopping street. The room is long and quite low,
extending to a tiny courtyard at the back that seats eight.

Inside, the original stone walls have been left exposed, and
pastel tablecloths soften the effect, making it a very pleasant
place to eat.

The salads are very fresh and you simply choose a small or
large plate and help yourself to the seven or eight on display.
There are also quiches and a couple of simple, non-meat, hot
main courses, such as courgette and tomatoes with peanut
sauce, vegetable curry, lasagne, lentil and ginger casserole.

Apart from the vegetarian element, they cook in a health-
conscious way, using wholefoods, and very little sugar and fat in
their pudding recipes. On display was a fairly solid-looking
slimmers' cake following these principles. I went for the fresh
blackberry and apple crumble, which had a nice, slightly sour
tang just to my liking.

Apart from the food on offer you can indulge in the Whole
Health Package. Elizabeth Arnold, who runs Nutters, has been
trained in massage and as a fitness instructor. She has a therapy
room for relaxation massage, as well as links with the nearby
Health Club for fitness programmes and saunas. All in all it
sounds a lovely way to spend the day.

Open: 9.30-6 Tuesday-Saturday
Credit cards: none
40 seats
 ♿ ｜○｜ 🚭 section

Twenty One, The Square

21 The Square, Potton, nr Sandy, Bedfordshire SG19 2NP
☎ 0767 261656
🏠 £14

This restaurant is set in a charming Georgian house with the interior design reflecting the exterior. There are heavy, gilt mirrors, and a pleasing colour scheme of cream, green and peach.

There is a set three-course meal that changes once a month. Usually there are four starters that are suitable for vegetarians and two of these are vegan. All the soups are thoughtfully made with vegetable stock, to save confusion. There might also be deep-fried Brie with fresh fruit sauce, tabbouleh, or a summer vegetable jelly of dry white wine (using agar). I was impressed by the fact that, although neither of those responsible for the food were vegetarian they were well aware of the requirements.

The main courses are imaginative and pleasantly served. There is the unusual Chinese potato cake with marrow and dates, pasta with a red wine sauce and seasonal vegetables, spinach and lentil roulade or cheese and asparagus charlotte.

To follow, there are some delicious puddings.

The ambience is relaxing and the service professional, making it a good place for a rather special meal.

Open: 7-9.30 (last orders) Tuesday-Saturday
35 seats

Upstairs Downstairs

1-2 Waxhouse Gate, High Street, St Albans, Hertfordshire AL3 4EW

☎ 0727 54843

🏠 £7

This is a friendly restaurant, tucked away down a small lane leading to St Albans Abbey. The interior of Upstairs Downstairs has a Dickensian feeling with some interesting antiques and paintings.

There are always three vegetarian main courses on the menu, and these change daily. The cooking is international so starters can be quite exotic — such as avocado and raspberry coulis — and you might find a choice of roulade, green bean curry or mushroom and aduki croquettes.

There is an informal atmosphere here, and it's a good place for a pleasant night out.

Open: 10-3, 6.30-10.30 daily
45 seats

      section

Heart of England

Gloucestershire, Hereford and Worcester, Shropshire, Staffordshire, Warwickshire, West Midlands

Of the places reviewed in this area, surprisingly few are wholly vegetarian, but those included here are certainly offering a great deal more than the ubiquitous quiche.

All the hotels mentioned have imaginative and quite extensive menus for vegetarians — often very reasonably priced. When you eat at these places you get the benefit of comfortable surroundings and professional service. The pubs, too, have responded to the demand for vegetarian food.

Generally I found the prices in this area reasonable and wholefoods used extensively.

There are some well-established vegetarian (or nearly veggie) places, too, that are of a good standard, particularly in Shrewsbury and Ludlow. These towns, interesting in themselves with their great border castles, are surrounded by marvellous unspoiled countryside, which it's well worth taking several days to explore.

There are some small eating places such as Olivers at Ironbridge that are certainly worth a visit. Sadly the more touristy area around Stratford is really lacking in good vegetarian eating places, though Birmingham offers a good choice. Worth visiting, too, is Ryton Gardens, the centre for organic gardening.

Acorn Wholefood Restaurant

26 Sandford Avenue, Church Stretton, Shropshire, FY6 6BW
☎ 0694 722495
🏠 £4

This is a straightforward little establishment, run by a couple
who want to provide wholefoods, but have found that it does
take time to build up the business. They give you a friendly
welcome and the place is clean and simple — the menu is
simple too.
   Starters include humus, and mushroom soup, the main
courses are chilli or vegetable lasagne, with salads, and you can
order home-made cakes and fresh fruit puddings. Although they
are not licensed, you can bring your own wine if you want to.
   It's very good value and certainly deserves to survive. Weather
permitting, you can eat outside, too.

Open: 9.30-5.30 Monday-Saturday, 10-6.30 Sunday
         (will take party bookings for Fridays and Saturdays)
Credit cards: none
40 seats

🗐 🚭 section

Baker's Arms

Broad Campden, Chipping Campden, Gloucester, GL5 6UR
☎ 0386 840515
🏠 £5

Broad Campden is typical of many Cotswold villages with its straight, sweeping main street, flanked by sandstone buildings. The high street here is particularly wide, hence the origin of the name perhaps, giving very easy access to modern-day coaches, which sadly means that it tends to be a rather overcrowded place during the high season.

It is good to find a pub where, as a vegetarian, you don't get stuck with a ploughman's! The food served at the Baker's Arms is a little more varied with main-course choices, such as vegetarian cottage pie, mushroom crêpes à la crème, vegetarian chilli and a very tasty mushroom and nut fettucini. The portions are quite small, but they leave you room for the traditional style puddings of cherry flan, apple pie and apricot crumble. Do check on the ingredients of these at the time as they do vary.

In summer it is possible to spill out into the garden, and in winter, the pub has a cosy feel to it with the dark wooden interior, old beam and stone floors. The service is good and the staff friendly when they are not too rushed.

Open: 12-9.45, summer, 12-2, 7-9.45, winter
Credit cards: none
40 seats, plus garden

♿ 🍾 ▱ ⊖

Corse Lawn House Hotel

Corse Lawn, Gloucester, GL19 4LZ
☎ 045278 479
🛏 £18 evening, £12 day

The present hotel at Corse Lawn, built in the Queen Anne period, was a well-known staging post between Worcester and Gloucester. Although close to both the M5 and M50, the village itself is in a most attractive unspoilt area of Gloucestershire.

Corse Lawn House Hotel is an ideal place to have a very special night out. You can choose to eat in the elegant restaurant and have the set menu or have a lighter meal in the equally charming bar.

The restaurant is formal with smartly dressed professional staff in attendance. There is a full vegetarian menu with several choices at each course. Overall, the food is rich and some of the dishes imaginative. For starters there might be a cauliflower and mint soup, stuffed avocado or vol-au-vent of quail's eggs. The more unusual main courses comprise terrine of vegetables with a *beurre blanc sauce*, avocado with courgettes, chestnuts and noodles, and a rich but delicate *feuilleté* of wild mushrooms. There is also an irresistible dessert trolley with a huge selection to choose from.

The set evening menu is quite pricey, but this is to be expected for a place of this calibre. However, a similar menu is offered at lunch-time for a very reasonable £11.50.

An alternative is to eat in the bar, where they offer some of the dishes that feature on the main restaurant menu, but you don't need to have all the courses. In addition, there are some excellent salads available here. The bar is smart, but very cosy, and a certain standard of dress is expected even though the atmosphere is less formal than in the restaurant.

Open: 12-2, 7-10 daily
50 restaurant, 40 bar seats

Down to Earth Wholefoods and Vegetarian Restaurant ✓

11 The Forum, Eastgate Shopping Centre, Gloucester,
GL1 1VG
☎ 0452 305832
🏠 £5

Down to Earth is tucked away in part of an indoor market complex and you'll find the entrance in Eastgate Market. It's typical of the stripped pine casual eating places that are nevertheless good value. Generally the food is fresh as everything is cooked on the premises.

There's a fairly predictable menu of nut roast, moussaka or lasagne served with two veg for under £3 and a range of salads.

The menu remains quite similar through the year, with a few seasonal changes. In the winter you'll find some rib-sticking puddings, such as traditional apple pie or bread-and-butter pudding, or summer delights of cream pavlova.

Open: 9-4.30 Monday-Saturday
Credit cards: none
40 seats

Evesham Hotel

Coopers Lane, Evesham, Worcestershire WR11 6DA
☎ 0386 765566
🏠 £15

Evesham is an interesting place to visit with its historic
buildings and a pleasant river walk. It is the site of a famous
battle in 1265 where Prince Edward and supporters defeated
Simon De Montfort. Sadly all that remains of this particular
piece of history is a scruffy piece of land just off the A435.

The Evesham Hotel merits a mention for its alcoholic
eccentricities as much as its imaginative vegetarian food! While
there is indeed a wine list, it features no French or German
wines, and the choice of liqueurs is fantastic with at least 150
varieties listed. So, you would most likely need to become a
devoted regular to get through the whole range. But you needn't
just rely on the drinks to make your visit to this restaurant
worthwhile — the vegetarian menu is good and the style of
cooking creative.

There are several starters, consisting of avocado and cheese
mousse, cambozola cheese fritters and a refreshing paw paw and
lychee salad. The one main course changes each night, so you
can check it appeals in advance. We had a light but rich filo
pastry dish. The whole thing was built up in layers and filled
with a memorable pistachio and carrot mousse. Other recent
main-course specials have been stuffed mushrooms, moistened
with white wine and served with cream sauce, wholemeal rice
cutlets or broccoli and brazil nut *croustade*. There are a good
range of puddings and home-made ice-creams, too.

The restaurant is formal and very comfortable, the outlook
onto a pretty garden is most attractive and the service is
attentive and professional, though I find the gimmicky
presentation of the menu not to my taste. As well as making a
good place for a special evening out, this restaurant makes a
splendid venue for a party.

Open: 12.30-2, 7-9.30 daily
60 seats

116

George Rafters

42 Castle Hill, Kenilworth, Warwickshire, CV8 1NB
☎ 0926 52074
🏠 £10

This pretty restaurant is one of the Bobby Brown's Collection, which owns several places around Birmingham and in Warwickshire.

George Rafters is in an attractive terrace house opposite Kenilworth Castle. The interior has a Laura Ashley, Victorian feel with blue and apricot furnishings, pine dresser and interesting reproduction prints.

The menu changes about every two to three months, and there is usually a choice of two vegetarian main courses, but the number of starters will vary. When we visited it was only possible to have a cream cheese dip with crudites. The present menu has at least three starters: Brie with gooseberry sauce, Stilton and walnut salad, and pink grapefruit laced with rum and grilled. The main courses follow predictable lines of lasagne and chilli without meat, but they also do an interesting bulgur wheat casserole. The food was tasty and well served. Puddings are rich, sweet or creamy.

This is a good venue for a smart lunch or a place for an evening out with a party of mixed eating requirements.

Open: 12-2, 7-10.30 Monday-Saturday, 12.30-2.30, 7-10.30
　　　Sunday
40 seats

Gingers

7a High Street, Kings Heath, Birmingham
☎ 021-444 0906
£8

Gingers is housed in a late-Victorian building that was once part of a pub. The owners have tried to give the interior a period feel with a small print, Laura Ashley-style wallpaper, open fireplace and richly coloured decor with dark green tablecloths.

There is an à la carte menu that changes completely about four times a year, though individual dishes do change from time to time. The choice is quite good with four starters, six main courses and always choices for vegans (or some dishes that can be prepared minus a cheese topping, say, for you). In addition there is always a daily special chalked up on the board.

The food is quite simple, with a strong reliance on wholefoods, such as beans, lentils and pasta. Starters include a simple soup, pâté, humus and garlic mushrooms (served cold and very garlicy). Some of the main dishes are quite heavy-going, so choose carefully if these are not to your taste. All the food is well presented, looks attractive on the plate and often comes with nice side-salads.

We had an excellent ratatouille with black-eye beans, which had a good spicy sauce, and a very good moussaka. Again these were well-flavoured and packed with a nice mixture of ingredients. Our other choices of aduki bean pasta and cashew paella were not so successful. The pasta was bland and the paella soggy. However, the chap on the next table, eating the same dish, sent his compliments to the chef!

The puddings tend to have a cake bias with Swiss carrot cake, banana and coffee cake and honey cake. There was also a rather dull-sounding dairy ice-cream, that turned out to be delicious and very creamy. We finished with good coffee and, surprisingly, chocolate wafer mints!

The meal at Gingers (assuming you like what you have chosen) is good value and the surroundings are very pleasing. If you don't like the meal, it is probably worth having a second go.

Open: 6-9 (last orders) Monday-Saturday
Credit cards: none
40 seats

  ♿ 📖 🚫 section

The Good Life Wholefood Restaurant

Barracks Passage, 73c Wyle Cop, Shrewsbury, Shropshire,
SY1 1XA
☎ 0743 50455
🏠 £3

Tucked away in one of the many quaint passages in Shrewsbury
is this pleasant, efficiently run, family restaurant. It is of the
stripped pine school of decor, clean and homely.

The daily menu is chalked up on the blackboard and you help
yourself. There is everything you would expect in this type of
establishment. There is a different soup daily, plus the choice of
wholemeal quiches such as mushroom and tomato, cheese and
sweetcorn, and broccoli and Stilton. Jacket spuds come plain or
filled and there may be as many as eight different salads. 'Hot
specials' are quite basic, such as beany ratatouille or egg
Florentine, but are well prepared and tasty.

Plenty more tempting items follow, which are equally good
value. Chocolate rum and raisin pie, pavlova and lemon cream
flan will certainly satisfy anyone with a sweet tooth. There are
also, however, many plainer, different wholefood cakes, scones
and flapjacks to satisfy those of you with less sugary tastes, all
to be washed down with a good choice of drinks.

The Good Life Wholefood Restaurant lives up to its name and
makes an excellent place for day-time snacks for a full lunch.

Open: 9.30-3.30 Monday-Friday, till 4.30 Saturday
Credit cards: none
64 seats

🍾 🍽 🚭 section

The Grapevine Hotel

Sheep Street, Stow-on-the-Wold, Gloucestershire, GL54 1AU
☎ 0451 30344
🛏£13

'Dine at the Vine and you'll be agreeably surprised', says the literature — the odd *real* vine leaf tumbling onto the table!

The Grapevine Hotel is a delightful, small hotel in picturesque Stow-on-the-Wold, run by Sandra Elliot. She provides a full vegetarian menu and you have plenty of time to make up your mind, seated on deep, comfortable sofas in a cosy lounge, complete with log fire on colder days. The food is nicely cooked and well presented.

We had a delicious mushroom millefeuille, which consisted of a creamy mushroom and garlic sauce in a light puff pastry. There was also Stroganoff, vegetable papiotte (little parcels of vegetables cooked with white wine and herbs), lasagne, stuffed peppers or stir-fried vegetables. The accompanying vegetables came attractively arranged on a side plate. There were some starters and a good range of desserts. All in all, a most relaxing place to dine.

During the lunch-time period, only bar snacks are available, but there is often one dish suitable for vegetarians. The restaurant, which has recently been expanded, is elegant, beautifully furnished with a tasteful decor of soft pinks, greys and blues and subtle lighting.

Open: 12-2, 7-9.30 daily
60 seats

Hardwicks

2 Quality Square, Ludlow, Shropshire, SY8 1AR
☎ 0584 6470
 £4

This is a charming restaurant set in a quiet old precinct off the main square. The menu is small but distinctive, changing daily. For starters, there is home-made soup (but do check it is vegetarian as very occasionally chicken stock is used) and there are four vegetarian main courses. Many of the recipes are imaginative and there is a strong reliance on fresh vegetables.

We had the Swedish cabbage bake, flavoured with caraway, and topped with cheese. It tasted delicious. You might also find Mexican pepper casserole, spinach and mushroom soufflé, leek croustade or the intriguing mystery mushroom casserole.

All the main courses come with a choice of two salads, which again vary considerably depending on what is in season.

For pudding, there are some marvellous dessert cakes, made using fresh fruit, that can be served either hot or cold. These are special recipes unique to Hardwicks. Some traditional puds, such as crumble or pie are often on the menu as well.

This is a lovely place to have lunch — and cakes — throughout the day. If you get the right weather, there are 12 places to sit outside, too.

Open: 10-5 Monday-Saturday, till 4.30 November-Easter,
      closed Christmas week
Credit cards: none
35 seats

🕯 ✐ 🚭 section

Jules

Broad Street, Weobley, Hereford, HR4 8SB
☎ 0544 318206
🏠 £9

Weobley is well worth a visit and not just for the food. It is one of England's most attractive villages, with the majority of the buildings being black and white half-timbered.

Jules is on the edge of the main village square. The interior is quite dark and bistro-like, with high, wooden booths dividing the eating area. In the day you can drop in for a casual lunch or afternoon tea, but it is necessary to book for the evening meals.

The menu remains roughly the same all day, though there is a slightly bigger choice in the evenings. Usually there are a few suitable starters, but probably only one vegetarian main course. The accent is on wholefoods, although white flour is used for both bread and pastry.

We had a substantial lentil, carrot and coriander soup as a starter, served with a crusty (white) cottage roll. The main course was filling too, but very tasty: butter beans, leek and apple casserole with cider that came with roast potatoes and cauliflower cheese. We made room though for the delicious apple and cinnamon pie with home-made pistachio ice-cream.

There was no one about when we went in and you need to ring the bell for attention. Sadly the service was a little offhand, although the food did make up for this to a certain extent.

It is useful to know that they also do bed and breakfast although I didn't see the rooms.

Open: 12-2 (lunch) 2-5 (tea) 7.30-10 daily
36 seats

La Santé

182 High Street, Harborne, Birmingham, B17 9PP
☎ 021-426 4133
🏠 £7

You might not expect there to be such a thing as a *French* vegetarian restaurant as the terms seem self-contradictory, but La Santé is just such a place, and authentic too.

Owned by a Frenchman, with a French manager and French waiter and, of course, French menu that is, interestingly, a mixture of wholefood and non-wholefood dishes. For starters there was *soupe au fenouil, beignets au fromage* or crudites, and a choice of six or seven main courses. These ranged from the more predictable raclette, crêpes, and *fondu savoyarde* to *timbale farcie de legumes* and *stroganoff (French?) de legumes*. There were some delicious accompanying vegetables as well as the classic green salad.

Pudding were sorbets, ice-creams, and apple *tarte* as well as a *plateau de fromage*.

Everything we had was very tasty and well presented. The service was friendly and efficient. The Frenchness of the place certainly adds a special dimension, giving you that sense of style which makes dining out here quite special.

Open: 7-10 Tuesday-Saturday
40 seats

The Loose Box Restaurant

18 High Street, Stratford-upon-Avon, Warwickshire,
CV37 6AU
 0789 204999
 £7

It has struck me as odd in the past that places clearly geared up
to plenty of tourism are less aware of changing tastes, and it is
often in these towns that I've had to resort to the standard
Italian or Indian meal just to get something veggie. At last,
however, there is somewhere in Stratford where they advertise
that they specialize in vegetarian (and fish) dishes and, although
they are not exceptional, they are more than acceptable.

The restaurant is on the main high street. Inside it is nicely
decorated, with wooden booths, and good use of pretty fabric.

We tried a celeriac, Stilton and port pâté, served with hot
toast. The pâté had both a good texture and flavour, and a
cream of wild mushroom soup was nice, if a little floury.

There were three main courses to choose from. The red kidney
bean and okra casserole was well flavoured, but the sauce was
more of a juice than a sauce. The desserts were uninspiring.

Quibbles apart, do take advantage of their early opening hours
to refuel before the theatre.

Open: 12-2, 5.30-10 Monday-Friday (closed Saturday morning
      and lunchtime)
60 seats

Moran's Eating House

127 Bath Road, Cheltenham, Gloucestershire, GL53 7LS
☎ 0242 581411
🏠 £8

At the moment this large, casual restaurant is almost the only place in Cheltenham serving a good selection of vegetarian food. Although the owner is not vegetarian, there are staff who are and they generally prepare the vegetarian menu.

Some dishes are permanently featured, but there are also three dishes that appear on the 'Specials' board and these change daily. You might be offered Mrs Moran's fruit and nut salad, *provençale* flan, or giant mushrooms stuffed with avocado, cashew and mango with curried tomato sauce. Many of the soups and starters are also suitable, including a delicious cauliflower and Stilton soup. There is a good choice of puddings — banana pancakes, raspberry sorbet and home-made cheesecake (usually gelatine-free).

This place does not advertise its vegetarian fare, but has recently found the need to increase its menu to cater for the demand. The decor is casual and modern so it makes a good place for lunch or an informal night out.

Open: 10.30-2.30 Tuesday-Saturday, 6.30-10.45 Monday-
        Saturday
Credit cards: none
120 seats

♿ 🍷 📋 ⊖

The Old School Restaurant

Staffordshire Peak Arts Centre, The Old School, Cauldon
Lowe, Staffordshire, ST10 3EX
☎ 0538 308431
🏠 £4

The wind certainly whistles round these old school buildings
and I should think many a child froze during play-time here!

Inside, the former hall, with its lofty ceiling, houses the
restaurant and a huge, solid-fuel fire soon dispels any chill. The
spacious room is cleverly divided up with wicker screens, and
the vast amount of wall space is taken up with all sorts of
original paintings, etchings, etc., that spill over from the craft
shop into the classrooms.

Lunches are served from midday. The food is tasty, even if the
quality of presentation is somewhat lacking. I had two excellent
nut burgers that had a very strong mushroom flavour, served
with a rather ordinary salad. The cashew and celery loaf was
coarsely textured, with a lovely lemon tang.

I had some moist carrot cake to follow and a gorgeous muesli
and orange cake was also on the menu.

The restaurant changed hands in 1988, and the new owners
are making changes to the menu.

Open: 10.30-5.30 Friday-Sunday January and February,
        daily March-Christmas
40 seats

The Old White Lion Inn

37 North Street, Winchcombe, Cheltenham, Gloucester,
GL54 5PS
☎ 0242 603300
🏠 £10

Vegetarian food hasn't been available for very long at the Old
White Lion, but now there is a small menu — nothing very
imaginative but certainly adequate.

   Starters consist of soup (do check it is vegetarian at the time),
egg mayonnaise and ratatouille. The main courses include
Stroganoff, chilli croquettes, lasagne and nut loaf. This menu
changes about every two months and they are gradually using
more wholefood, brown rice, etc. Apart from what is on offer,
they will cater for special diets with prior notice.

Open: 12-2.30, 7-onwards daily November-Easter, Winter —
      closed Sunday evenings and in January and February,
      closed Monday evenings.
48 seats

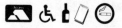

Olivers at Ironbridge

33a High Street, Ironbridge, Shropshire, TF8 7AG
☎ 0952 453086
£5

Upstairs at Olivers at Ironbridge, just a few minutes from the famous iron bridge itself, is this excellent small restaurant that describes itself as a vegetarian bistro. The pretty interior is enhanced by Victorian lighting and exposed beams. The tables are covered in attractive, green stripy linen tablecloths and the serving staff are dressed to match! The place is spotlessly clean, and the service is friendly but fairly leisurely.

The menu isn't anything out of the ordinary, but it is well prepared and well presented. Starters consist of a home-made soup of the day, corn on the cob, or vegetarian pâté and toast. Regular items on the menu include leek and Stilton flan, ratatouille, or cauliflower mornay. For lighter snacks there are baked potatoes with salad, cottage cheese or Boston baked beans. Don't forget to look at the blackboard which shows the daily 'Hot special'.

There are good home-made ice-cream and cakes to follow.

Olivers is also open in the evening. They change this menu daily and try to use as many fresh seasonal products as possible, using no frozen vegetables. They also use unrefined ingredients wherever appropriate and place an emphasis on wholefood cooking.

Olivers is a pleasant place for lunch if you are touring Shropshire, but it is also worth visiting in the evening if you want a casual meal out.

Open: 10.00-6.00 Tuesday and Wednesday, 7.30-11.30
        Thursday-Saturday
Credit cards: none
26 seats

The Park House Hotel and Restaurant

Park Street, Shifnal, Shropshire, TF11 9BA
☎ 0952 460128
🛏 £15

Thanks to a creative chef and forward-looking manager, there is a good and imaginative vegetarian menu on offer in all of the restaurants at the Park House Hotel. I dined in the Grill Room, a tastefully decorated room with warm colours, tables with elegant settings and a chance to eat in style and all the trimmings you normally associate with top-class restaurants.

There are dishes that are suitable on the regular menu, but there is also a completely separate list for vegetarians. On that menu there was chilled cucumber soup with fresh cream and mint, and fresh melon served in a delicate fan with blueberry and lime sauce. I had the giant mushrooms filled with Stilton, Brie and a tomato sauce, which were very tasty.

There were four different main courses. I had the seasonal vegetable crumble. The topping was a little salty for my taste, but the vegetables below tasted good. The pastry parcel with hazelnut purée, served with basil sauce was good. There was also a very mild curry of vegetables, served with rice. All the food is beautifully presented and a large choice of side vegetables are served separately.

The sweet trolley is a vision to behold. Good use was made of seasonal fruits to produce some delectable tartlets and purées. The fruit salad was splendid, not sweet and packed with exotica. There were gâteaux, cheesecakes and so on, but it is best to check on the gelatine content at the time. As everything is made on the premises, there should be no problem finding out. All the staff are extremely helpful.

The Park House Hotel and Restaurant is a a very good venue for a special night out, business dinners or lunches, or somewhere to go with a mixed party. Apart from the Grill Room, there is The Idsall Restaurant, which is more formal and expensive. Here too they have an extensive vegetarian menu.

This hotel is part of Associated Leisure Hotels Ltd. (061-941 6848) and they have 10 hotels round the country, which may be well worth investigating. I understand though that menus are planned by the individual managers and chefs in each hotel. I

hope more of them will follow the example of Park House, if
they do not already do so.

Open: 12.30-2.30, 6.30-9.30 (last orders) daily
60 seats

Ryton Gardens Café

National Centre for Organic Gardening, Ryton-on-Dunsmore,
Coventry, CV8 3LG
☎ 0203 303517
🏠 £5

Even I didn't recognize all the ingredients in the salad I had
here, which is hardly surprising as the Ryton Gardens Café is
part of the National Centre for Organic Gardening, and they
make full use of a huge variety of unusual ingredients grown in
the gardens in their cooking. It is nearly all vegetarian, as
indeed are most of the staff.

Start with one of their home-made soups, which is always
vegetarian and comes with a roll and butter. For a main course,
there's likely to be a risotto or rice bake with green peppers,
stuffed pancakes, spinach roulade or vegetable crumble. There is
also a choice of savoury quiche or tart served with salad.

The puddings were lovely too, and, again, they use all their
organic produce. I had a deliciously light pear fool. Summer
pudding is a speciality when the fruit is in season. There were
also cakes and gâteaux. It's a good place for tea, as they serve
organic cream on wholemeal fruit scones.

The café, although small, is light and airy. You may have to
share tables when it gets busy. Not only can you look out at
the gardens, but there is some informative reading matter
around. The place had a very homely atmosphere and the credit
for that is due to the very friendly staff.

Do allow yourself time to browse around the shop and the
Gardens too. There are guided tours twice daily.

Open: 10-5 daily
28 seats inside, 48 patio

Stones Brasserie

Montpelier Courtyard, Cheltenham, Gloucestershire,
GL50 1UF
☎ 0242 527537
🏠 £7

Stones Brasserie is a reasonable place to get a quick lunch or
supper before a show.

The vegetarian choices are basic: garlic mushrooms for starters
and vegetable pie or pasta dishes as a main course. These come
served with a decent salad. More interesting is the pancake
stuffed with Chinese-style vegetables and the tasty goat's cheese
salad.

Fudge cake and other standard fare are for pudding.

You may not want to linger too long here though as the seats
are not very comfortable and the background music is rather
intrusive.

Open: 11-11 Monday-Thursday, 11-12 midnight Friday and
      Saturday, 12-4, 7-10.30 Sunday.
80 seats

The Sun Inn

Clun, Craven Arms, Shropshire, SY7 8JB
☎ 05884 559 or 277
🏨 £7

This is a delightful, small, unspoiled country pub, dating, as far
as the owners can discover, from the fifteenth century. Although
neither of the owners are vegetarian themselves, they ran a
vegetarian restaurant in Birmingham for several years and are
very well acquainted with the style of cuisine.

There is a set menu for vegetarians that only changes a couple
of times a year. There is a choice of three starters — soup, pâté
or something like garlic mushrooms — and a couple of main
courses — cashew paella (I was told it was Sarah Brown's!), and
a lentil and cheese bake. In addition, there is always a different
daily 'Special', such as Red Dragon Pie, or several unusual
Indian dishes. They make vegetarian koftas from green bananas
and these have proved very popular, as well as spicy black-eye
beans with coriander. These main courses come with salad, hot,
seasonal vegetables, and potatoes, either in their jackets or new
potatoes depending on the time of year.

Puddings also vary according to what fruit is available.
Plenty of apples were being used when we went in the autumn
for traditional pies and a lovely Jewish cheese and apple
cheesecake that could be eaten hot or cold. The menu is kept
small deliberately as they make everything themselves.

In the summer The Sun Inn is exceedingly popular, so it is
certainly worth booking a table in the little dining room. In the
winter there is more space and it's possible to enjoy both the
food and the welcoming open fires in relative peace.
Accommodation is also available.

Open: 12-2, 7-9 daily
Credit cards: none
50 seats
♿ 🍼 ▱ ☕

The Swan

Aston Munslow Nr Craven Arms, Shropshire, SY7 9ER
☎ 058476 271
🏠 £3

A good, well-run pub where the owners do the cooking.
Although the food is not vegetarian, they have found an
increasing demand for meatless meals.

They have tried various dishes and found that the most
popular are cauliflower cheese and a mixed bean hot-pot. The
hot-pot is a casserole of six different pulses, served in a mild
curry sauce, topped with wholewheat breadcrumbs and cheese.

The food is served in tasteful pottery and comes with granary
bread and salad garnish. It was simple but well prepared. They
also do ploughman's lunches, and have tried vegetarian pâtés.

At present you order at the bar and the food is brought to
you, but they have plans for some separate seating arrangements
and possibly smoking restriction.

Open: 12-2, 7-9 daily except Tuesday
Credit cards: none
40 seats

♿ 🍼 🚭 ☺

The Three Tuns

Salop Street, Bishops Castle, Shropshire, SY9 5BW
☎ 0588 638797
🏠 £5

This is a small, unspoiled pub that has a tremendous reputation for good food, and deservedly so.

The usual menu has soup, sometimes there is a choice and one will be vegetable-based whilst the other relies on a meat stock. Standard, hot, main courses are ratatouille and lasagne, but there will often be extra special dishes, such as moussaka. These can be augmented with a choice of breads — garlic, French or granary — or side-salads and jacket potatoes. if you are not so hungry, there is a good ploughman's lunch served.

Puddings follow fairly traditional lines with pies, crumbles and brandy fudge cake, but you may find carrot cake here too.

The prices are reasonable and, apart from the food, the beer is good too. They can get overwhelmed if things get too busy and, as a result, the vegetarian menu may well be more limited in the height of summer. I was there in May and there was a good choice then. They serve generous portions, the food was tasty and came with a decent salad of the green leaf kind. At the moment you need to order at the bar, and there is limited seating, but plans are afoot to make some changes.

Open: 12-2, 7-10 daily
Credit cards: none
25 seats in bar

🍾 ▱ ◓

Three Ways Hotel

Mickleton, Chipping Campden, Gloucester, GL55 65B
☎ 0386 438231
🛏 £11

This welcoming, friendly hotel, set in a typical Cotswold
building, is pleased to welcome non-residents. The professional
service is friendly and helpful, the decor traditional and
comfortable. The vegetarian food is usually tasty and is served
in very substantial portions. There are starters of avocado,
stuffed with an exceedingly rich Stilton and walnut cream, and
deep-fried mushrooms. The main course menu might include
mushroom Stroganoff with brown rice, stuffed aubergine or
vegetables *au gratin*. The side servings of vegetables are always
well prepared.

Beware the puddings! The Hotel is the home of the famous
'Pudding Club', which meets on the first Friday of the month
between September and April. Booking — and loose clothes —
are essential. At these meals, the savouries are merely an aperitif
before sampling at least seven traditional English puddings.
Vegetarians please note that fortunately or unfortunately at least
five of the seven are suet-free, so you indulge along with
everyone else!

Open: 12-2 daily, 12.30-2 Sunday, 7-9 Sunday-Thursday, till
　　　9.30 Friday and Saturday
80 seats

The Unicorn Vegetarian Restaurant and Coffee Shop ✓

Wyle Cop, Shrewsbury, Shropshire, SY1 1XB
☎ 0743 66890
£3 day, £7 evening

The Unicorn Vegetarian Restaurant is in a lovely building, formerly a pub, with oak panelling, open fires and pine tables. Often the walls are hung with paintings by local artists.

The menu in the day-time is reasonably priced and there is an emphasis on simple meals and quick snacks so people can nip in in their lunch hours and get a decent bite to eat. There is soup, pâté, dips, and snacks such as cheesy nut burgers with a home-made bun, pickle or mayonnaise, and pizza. For more serious eating there are two or three 'Hot specials' such as Chinese parsnip and mushroom crumble, where the vegetables are cooked in ginger and mustard to give them a distinctive flavour. There might also be a casserole (spicy cauliflower and pinto bean, for example) and some type of loaf or bake served with a sauce. There are several salads to choose from and you can have either a mixed bowlful or individual portions. Each salad comes with a flavoursome dressing, such as sesame or garlic.

To follow there are home-made ice-creams and sorbets, plus a good selection of cakes and slices.

In the evenings the menu remains the same in principle, but the dishes tend to be a little more expensive and exotic, though you can still have a really good meal and plenty of change from £10.

You feel here that the owners care about the quality of the food, avoiding harmful E-numbers wherever possible, making everything themselves, right down to the bread and making sure that there is a choice for vegans on each course. They set themselves high standards, which they certainly live up to.

Open: 10-5 Monday and Tuesday, 7-11 Wednesday-Saturday
Credit cards: none
40 seats

The Wharf Restaurant

Froghall Wharf, Foxt Road, Froghall, Stoke-on-Trent,
Staffordshire, ST10 2HJ
☎ 053 871 486
🏠 £14

The Wharf Restaurant is a real gem, set by the side of the
Caldon canal in the heart of the Staffordshire countryside. The
canal is complete with its own narrow boat and horse. Sadly
there is not a view of that once you are inside the restaurant,
but it scarcely matters as you then really need to concentrate on
the marvellous food.

The owners hail from Portsmouth but fell in love with the
place, and it shows — not only in the quality of the dishes
produced, but the way in which this 200-year-old warehouse has
been painstakingly restored. The brickwork has been properly
cleaned so it is now a splendid feature and is nicely offset with
lots of varnished wood. The restaurant is quite formal, with
elegant tableware and comfortable furniture.

The menu changes every three months and starters might
include an appropriately-named water lily timbal with asparagus
sauce, poached pear with Stilton, or mushroom and hazelnut
soup. Sorbet follows, to clear the palate and then there are two
choices for a main course: a layered terrine or vegetable kebabs.
The food was first class and it is refreshing to have a vegetarian
meal that isn't a cheese-laden lasagne. Vegans can be catered for
too with prior notice. But here's a piece of one-upmanship —
literally: if you ask in advance, you can have the whole meal
served up to you on a three-and-a-half hour canal trip.

You'll find The Wharf Restaurant just outside Froghall village
on the A52.

Open: 11-5, 7.30 onwards (last orders 9.15) Tuesday-Saturday
       Spring Bank Holiday — September 11-5, Thursday-
       Sunday
40 seats

The Wheatsheaf Inn

Oaksey, Nr Cirencester, SN16 9TB
☎ 06667 348
🏠 £4

Good food, in generous portions, is served in The Wheatsheaf —
a pleasant village pub. The menu suitable for vegetarians is
quite small and doesn't change frequently. There is a choice of
aduki pie, moussaka, and vegetable curry — all served with a
decent green salad *and* jacket potato if you're really hungry, as
we were!

   You order your food at the bar and your meal is then brought
to your table quickly. The tasty moussaka was piping hot and
attractively served. To follow, there are some fairly traditional
puddings, such as apple pie and banana split. It is probably
best to check on the ingredients of these before ordering.

   The village of Oaksey is off the A429 between Cirencester and
Malmesbury.

Open: 12-2.30, 7-10 (no food served on Monday)
Credit cards: none
50 seats

♿ 🍷 🗔 😊

Wild Oats

5 Raddlebarn Road, Selly Oak, Birmingham, B29 6HJ
☎ 021-471 2459
🏠 £5 day, £6 evening

This vegetarian restaurant has a rustic feel to it with the wooden furniture and warm colour scheme. The menu is very basic and remains the same day and night — one soup, one casserole, one bake, and one quiche! The ingredients do change, however, and, although the format doesn't sound very inspiring, some of the dishes such as pasticcio or stuffed cabbage are quite adventurous. There are several salads to choose from as well as baked potatoes.

For puddings there are some home-made ice-creams, cheesecake, fruit fool and sometimes a slice of pie. You can bring your own wine too, as they are not licensed, as long as you pay a corkage fee.

The food is good value and wholesome.

Open: 12-2, 6-9 Tuesday-Saturday
Credit cards: none
30 seats

Ye Olde Inn

Winchcombe Road, Guiting Power, Nr Cheltenham,
Gloucestershire, GL54 5UX
☎ 04515 392
🏠 £5

Guiting Power is a delightful village. It certainly makes a good
place to have lunch, enjoy the area and local walks.

Ye Olde Inn is a welcoming, friendly pub, run by a
Scandinavian couple, that is certainly trying to give vegetarians
some good alternatives and develop more ideas in response to
demand.

The decor is plain but comfortable. You order your food at the
bar, and, once you have eaten, the plates are quickly cleared
away.

We had a tasty butter bean casserole that was served with an
unusual sweet-and-sour red cabbage, probably influenced by
Swedish cuisine. The combination of flavours worked really well.
There was also vegetable curry, served with brown rice, plus
some fresh salads and hot vegetables.

The puddings are all home-made and you can choose from
apple crumble, coffee fudge pudding and lovely, sweet crêpes,
filled with cheese, nuts and honey. The whole meal is good
value.

Open: 12-1.45, 6.45-9 Tuesday-Friday, 12-1.45, 6.45-9.30
      Saturday and Sunday
Credit cards: none
24 seats

♿ 🍾 📋 ☕

East Midlands

Derbyshire, Nottinghamshire, Lincolnshire, Leicestershire

Despite being in the centre of the country, I feel this area has a rather forgotten feel to it, not least in terms of the amount and quality of vegetarian food on offer.

There is some beautiful countryside to explore, especially the Southern Peak District around Bakewell, Ashbourne and the grand spa town of Buxton. There are many other interesting places between Southwell, which is England's smallest cathedral town, and Lincoln, with its very grand hill-top cathedral. Country towns such as Oundle, Melton Mowbray and Stamford, which seems brimming with elaborate buildings are lovely, too. It is a pity, though, that these places have little or nothing out of the ordinary to offer vegetarians.

In the region as a whole, there isn't an outstanding strictly vegetarian restaurant, though thankfully there are a couple of places that make a good effort to serve imaginative non-meat dishes, namely The Druid Inn and Knightingales.

Caudwell's Mill

Rowsley, Nr Bakewell, Derbyshire, DE4 2EB
☎ 0629 733185
🏠 £3

Caudwell's Mill is a complex of craft workshops, a working waterpowered mill, and the country parlour, which is a small, simple wholefood café. The buildings are attractive, though the interior of the café was rather sparse and lacking in atmosphere. However, the food was fine and extremely cheap.

The range is limited to standard fare with more choice on busier weekend days. Everything is made on the premises using the freshly milled flour. There are quiches and salads, savoury bakes, such as courgette and cauliflower or aubergine and mushroom, and sometimes lasagne.

The selection of wholemeal cakes was good. We had a lovely piece of cinnamon and apricot layer with herbal tea and the usual fruit juices, and then spent a happy hour wandering round the excellent craft shop, and of course took home a bag of flour.

Open: 10-6 daily, weekends only January and February, 10-4
      October-March
Credit cards: none
30 seats

♿ 🍴 ◎ 🚭

The Druid Inn

Birchover, Nr Matlock, Derbyshire DE4 2BL
☎ 062-988 302
🏠 £7

This lovely country pub is set in the heart of some beautiful
Derbyshire countryside, near Matlock, Bakewell and Chatsworth
House, where even nature seems to have been enhanced by
Capability Brown.

There is a very good range of vegetarian food at this friendly
and efficiently run place. You are advised to go early as it is
deservedly popular and, inevitably, can get smoky. We arrived
spot on 12 noon, but the bar was already getting busy.

There is a huge blackboard advertising the day's fare and as
things sell out they get rubbed off. You need to order from the
bar and say which room you are sitting in. There's a choice of
the bar itself, cosy and dark wood, or two more formal seating
areas — the restaurant room and the garden room (both rather
over furnished but quite pretty).

I had the aubergine pâté as a starter, which was light and very
lemony, served with granary-style French bread. Also on the
menu were a rich port and Stilton pâté and tomato and
vegetable soup.

The vegetable casserole as a main course was terrific. The very
lightly cooked vegetables — a really colourful mixture with corn,
broccoli and beans — were all hidden under a tasty tomato
sauce. Other choices were almond risotto with a peanut and
honey sauce, spinach roulade, fruit and vegetable curry and
Chinese vegetables in a sweet and sour sauce. All the food was
presented well with fresh salad garnishes.

You can book the tables in the dining rooms, which is
certainly advisable on weekend evenings.

Open: 12-2, 7-9.30 daily
114 seats

🅰 ♿ 🍴 📝 🚭

Green Apple

Diamond Court, Water Street, Bakewell, Derbyshire,
DE4 WL
☎ 062-981 4404
🏠 £5 day, £11 evening

Green Apple is quite tucked away on a corner of Bakewell's one-way system. The entrance is a short walk down an alleyway to a pretty courtyard. We were nicely greeted, shown to a table and asked if we wanted drinks before the meal. They do try here to add a sense of sophistication and occasion to your evening out with nice cloths on the tables, classical music playing and the sugar pink decor.

The soup we tried — tomato and apple — was a very pleasant starter and not too sweet. There are a couple of vegetarian choices for main courses. We had the aubergines with noodles, as the other dish on offer was a stuffed, baked potato, which seemed rather dull. The aubergines were disappointing, however. They were *warm* rather than *hot* and overladen with a seed and breadcrumb mixture. I felt they needed a good dollop of sauce. To make up for it though, the range of hot vegetables was good — carrots, turnips, cauliflower and jacket potato, ample for several people. Not feeling quite that hungry, I had a side-salad, which turned out to be a strange mixture of cooked peas, lemon pieces and olives. I would have preferred something raw. On my way up to choose a pudding, I noticed that all the salad mixtures were on the serving counter and I could easily have sent my salad back and got something more to my liking. I'll know next time I go!

The puddings are traditional concoctions of cream, fruit and soaked sponges, all wonderfully displayed and tempting.

During the day, the food is simpler and there is counter service.

Green Apple is quite acceptable for an evening out, and would suit parties of mixed eating habits especially. The non-vegetarians owners here are trying to learn more about vegetarian food from their vegetarian chef, and they do put on a very interesting Christmas menu.

Open: 11-2 Monday and Tuesday, 11-2, 7-10 Wednesday-
      Saturday
50 seats

146

Kinder Kitchen

3-5 Church Street, Hayfield, Derbyshire, SK12 5JE
☎ 0663 47321
🏠 £4 day £10 evening

This little restaurant was taken over early in 1988 when it already had established quite a reputation for its vegetarian food. The new owners have been anxious to carry on the tradition and have certainly maintained the high standards.

During the day, the food is light, with more snack-style items, such as vegeburgers, quiche and vegetarian soup, but there is always one 'Hot special' that is quite substantial, such as lasagne, which comes with salad and garlic bread. They also do traditional teas, and some good wholemeal cakes.

In the evening the mood changes, going up-market without being pretentious. The lighting is softened and the cosy room has a bistro feel. The evening menu changes monthly.

Of the five starters, there are always two that are vegetarian, such as courgette fritters with blue cheese dip, and a more predictable avocado with a fruit and nut filling in mayonnaise. Vegetarians will also find two choices for the main course, and sometimes an extra one chalked up on the blackboard. One month it was mushroom Stroganoff and vegetable moussaka, another it was hazelnut loaf and broccoli and leek *croustade*. The food is nicely cooked and very tasty.

For desserts there are gâteaux, such as chocolate brandy cake, ice-creams and sorbet, and old-fashioned puds such as apple crumble. All these are home-made.

I thought Kinder Kitchen was a very friendly place and the staff are clearly interested in pleasing customers. I had high tea as the restaurant was fully booked for the evening, but I am looking forward to going back.

Open: 10-5 Wednesday-Sunday, 7-10 Thursday-Saturday
40 seats

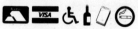

Knightingales

Guildhall Court, Guildhall Street, Grantham, Lincolnshire, NG31 6NJ
☎ 0476 79243
🏠 £3

Knightingales is an attractive, modern restaurant in a high-ceilinged building that used to be a wine warehouse. Thanks to good lighting and warm paintwork, the black and white interior, tiled floor and stainless steel serving counter appears smart rather than stark, and the staff give you a friendly welcome, even though when we went, we rushed in at 4.30, asking for soup!

A blackboard behind the counter lists the day's dishes. The soup was tomato, lentil and cumin, and there are several savouries to choose from, such as lasagne, vegetable bakes and flans, plus several salads.

We had a good fruit salad (much more fruit than juice) and a sweet but tasty apple and mincemeat pie to follow.

The portions are generous and the food is good value.

Open: 9.30-4.30 Monday-Saturday
Credit cards: none
48 seats

♿ 🍴 🍽 ☕

Monsal View Café

Monsal Head, Nr Bakewell, Derbyshire
☎ 062987 346
🏠 £3

The Monsal Dale viaduct was built in 1863 to carry the Midland line from London to Macclesfield. This particular section of the line was closed just over a century later, but it is now possible to walk nearly eight miles along the track and enjoy some beautiful scenery, extolled as 'Little Switzerland' by historic railway publicity.

Monsal Head is a fine viewing point, and also a good stopping place for refreshments.

The Monsal View Café is in what used to be a ticket office and railway worker's cottages which have been knocked into one. The interior has been well restored, using old cast-iron pillars to support the roof, and the walls are hung with enamel advertisements. Much of the furniture is dark-stained wood. The whole place has an attractive atmosphere.

We had a lentil crumble, which was quite salty but tasty nevertheless, which a jacket potato and a very plain but fresh salad. Vegetarians could also have savoury flan or sliced brown bread sandwiches.

Some of the cakes are wholefood and we indulged in an excellent carrot cake.

Open: 11-6 daily Easter-end October, weekends only
       November-Easter
Credit cards: none
35 seats

♿ 🍾 📋 🚭

Ritas

15 Goose Gate, Hockley, Nottinghamshire, NG1 1FE
☎ 0602 481115
🏠 £3

This small café is above Hiziki, the wholefood co-operative on Goose Gate. It is worth a mention mainly because the food offered is entirely vegan. This and the prices clearly appeal mostly to younger people (or perhaps I just suddenly felt older on my visit!)

There are usually a couple of hot main courses, such as vegetarian shepherd's pie or tempeh cutlets. I tried a tofu and cashew nut stir-fry with rice and spinach. Everything but the leathery tofu was great. The wheat and vegetable stew was plain and could have been more carefully flavoured. Decent bread and spread was available.

The fruit juices came in huge glasses, and seemed very cheap. The café is not licensed but you can bring alcohol in from the shop downstairs if you feel like something stronger.

The staff were fairly friendly, the atmosphere laid back and somewhat smoky.

Downstairs, the shop is very well stocked and they do a range of take-aways of variable quality. We had a couple of good cakes, a dull pasty, and a tasty bean and cheese pie, which may have tasted particularly good to me because of the six-hour mountain run I had just completed!

Open: 10-5 Monday-Saturday
Credit cards: none
40 seats

Ten

10 Commerce Square, The Lace Market, Nottingham,
Nottinghamshire, NG1 3DT
☎ 0602 585211
 £7

This is a pleasant restaurant in a converted basement. The
exposed painted pipes and plenty of plants make a nice
environment with a relaxed feel.

The service is on the slow side when things are busy, but,
while waiting for our meal, we were given a plate of crudites and
a dip to while away the time — a nice touch.

Starters include the usual soups and pâtés, such as humus or
avocado and cashew. Good old vegetarian stand-bys, such as
lasagne and nut roast, are the main courses, but there are also
some more intriguing dishes borrowed from *haute cuisine*. How
about nut cutlet Diane with a sauce of French mustard, brandy
and cream? (At £7.50 this is one of the most expensive options,
but it is worth it.) The food we had was tasty and well
presented.

For pudding there is ice-cream, Greek yoghurt with nuts and
honey, fruit syllabub and chocolate mousse.

Altogether it is a good place to eat and very good if you go
with a party as you can create more of an atmosphere.

It is possible that they may open in the day-time in the not
too distant future so do phone for details.

Open: 5.30-11.15 Tuesday-Friday, 12-12 Saturday
Credit cards: none
48 seats

🍴 ▱ 🚭

East Anglia

Cambridgeshire, Norfolk, Suffolk, Essex

There are a delightful mixture of pubs and restaurants serving vegetarian food in this area. Many of these places are good because they have been set up by individuals interested in developing their own style in terms of the menu or decor.

Some of the restaurants included are quite new, and I do hope they will become established. Pubs in East Anglia are serving a good range of imaginative alternatives for vegetarians as well as real ale and good-quality wine.

Of the leading towns and cities in the area, the choice is variable. Certainly there is no shortage of eating places in Norwich, whereas Cambridge, despite its multitude of students, is surprisingly barren.

The best restaurant in this area I feel is The Chalice at Bury St Edmonds where there is excellent food, both for casual, day-time eating and for special occasion meals in the evening.

Brambles Café

16-20 Exchange Street, Norwich, NR1 2AT
☎ 0603 624350
🏠 £7

Brambles is a modern, bright café with a young feeling about the decor and a slick atmosphere.

The choice of vegetarian food in the evenings is particularly good, with the continental menu built around pasta dishes. There are several sauces, such as neapolitan or pesto, and more substantial dishes such as blue cheese and mushrooms with tagliatelli, vegetable lasagne, and Angry Pasta. This last dish is terrific, a house speciality and is, in fact, ravioli filled with ricotta and spinach, served with a hot pepper and wine sauce. There's a good beany salad as well as some greenery, and predictable gâteaux and cheesecakes to follow (check on the ingredients of these when you order).

The service is fast and efficient. They have kept their eyes open for changing trends and made a conscious effort to add more vegetarian ideas to the menu.

At lunch-time, although the choice is more limited, it is nevertheless very good value, especially the filled rolls. They also offer a hot main course along the lines of vegetable bake.

Brambles is ideal for a quick, decent lunch-time snack, and in the evenings for an early meal when you are off to the cinema.

Open: 9.30-11 Tuesday-Thursday, till 12.30 Friday and
      Saturday
60 seats
 section

The Buck Inn

The Street, Flixton, Bungay, Suffolk, NR35 INZ
☎ 0986 2382
🏨 £7

One feature of this traditional, homely country pub is their Sunday lunch: roast beef and all the trimmings. Vegetarians needn't feel outdone though as they can have the works with nut roast for their main course!

The food sold here is made by outside caterers, the quality is consistent and the prices very reasonable. Starters are not particularly memorable, with humus, melon, or grapefruit, but the range of main courses is excellent. Vegetable crumble, three bean curry, lentil shepherd's pie, macaroni and vegetable bake, and a very tasty haricot bean hotpot served with potatoes and salad. Less substantial meals, such as a ploughman's, are on the bar snacks menu.

Puds include arctic roll and trifle (it is wise to check ingredients), as well as good, fresh fruit sorbets and ice-cream.

This nice, unpretentious pub certainly makes an effort to please all the customers. It is also somewhere good for a family outing.

Open: 12-2, 7-10 daily
Credit cards: none
30 seats

♿ 🚼 📓 🚭

The Chalice Restaurant   √

28/29 Cannon Street, Bury St Edmunds, Suffolk, IP33 1JR
☎ 028475 4855
🏠 £8

This is a well-established vegetarian restaurant that has managed
to make a success of its evening as well as its day opening.

Day-time food is often quite simple with things that people
can eat in a hurry if they are just popping in during their lunch
break. There are soups, jacket potatoes and a couple of hot
specials for those who have more time. The menu changes daily.

Evening menus are more elaborate and change on a weekly
basis. They are very popular and it is probably necessary to
book at the weekends. Part of their success must be due to their
enthusiasm for the food served. They feel it should be really
enjoyable and really enjoyed. The service is professional and
knowledgeable without being pretentious.

We had mushrooms tartare (stuffed mushrooms, crisply fried
and served with fresh tartare sauce) and spicy pumpkin soup —
both delicious and reasonably priced. Following this we tried
Russian Pie — a light, wholemeal pastry, filled with hard-boiled
eggs, cabbage, sour cream and tarragon with a parsley sauce.
This was excellent and came with some leeks and whole roast
potatoes with mustard. Another main course was the Mexican
Spaghetti Squash — a most unusual main course, topped with
cheese and served with side vegetables, though you could have
salad if you wished which looked good.

The puddings were terrific. To give you just a hint of the
delights on offer, imagine fresh pineapple brûlée with a thin,
burnt sugar topping and caramellized oranges.

There is an extensive wine list with bin-end bargains, as well
as hot, spicy, mulled wine.

There is a cosy, warm look to the dining room, with the
exposed brickwork, old pine furniture and open log fire. It used
to be an old bakery so the original oven has been kept as an
interesting feature. Overall The Chalice Restaurant has a calm
and unhurried ambience, which helps you to enjoy the
imaginative, well prepared food.

Open:12-2.30, 7-9.30 Wednesday-Saturday
Credit cards: none
50 seats
  ♿ 🍾 ▯ 🚭 section

Chives

25A Smallgate, Beccles, Suffolk NR34 9ED
☎ 0502 717772
🏠 £5

It is good to see a solely vegetarian place making headway in a
small, off-the-beaten-track place such as Beccles. Chris and
Carol Osborne are succeeding, and I'm sure that is not just due
to the slightly twee 'hospitality is our speciality' notice outside.
No, the food is good, carefully cooked and well presented. The
Newcastle Brown Ale soup was wonderful — rich and chunky
with a heart-warming flavour, and served with superb
wholewheat bread. The same bread is used for the sandwiches,
which are excellent value and all the better for being able to
choose your own filling. There are huge bowls of humus served
with fresh pitta bread, and main courses that come in portions
to defeat the most gargantuan appetite. The Provençale
Vegetable Pie looked delicious, and there was also a good
cheese and wine sauce served with pasta. Snack ideas included a
quarter-pound vegetarian burger.

Try to save space for a slither of home-made ice-creams:
walnut and maple, or honey and brandy, or weigh in with an
unusual hot apple and almond cake.

Chives is small, but hopefully not too short of room to make
enough to keep going. Places like this are few and far between.
Well worth a visit.

Open: 12-2 and 7-10 in the winter
Credit cards: none
20 seats

♿ 🍾 📋 🚭

The Crown Hotel

High Street, Southwold, Suffolk, IP18 6DP
☎ 0502 722275
🛏 £12

The Crown Hotel, part of Adnams Wine Merchants Company, has an imposing exterior that belies the friendly welcome given inside. The restaurant is formal, with smart uniformed staff, and the bar is cosy with lots of old wood and tastefully decorated. The same food is served in both restaurant and bar, although the prices are a little lower in the bar and it is also possible there to have some selected wines by the glass.

The style of the cuisine is nouvelle (though the portions are reasonable) with traditional touches and seasonal variations.

Their soups are always delicious, served in pretty cream bowls on little stands. There are some nice combinations of ingredients such as tomato and apple. Other starters include a local goat's cheese with seasonal salad, black olives and chives, or avocado with beef tomatoes and pine nuts.

Nut cutlet, that butt of vegetarian humour, is one of the main courses, but it was excellent. There are four other main choices, including baked peppers, ratatouille with braised rice, and fresh vegetable and fruit *gratin*. There are some rich but light puddings, such as *fromage blanc* with orange sauce, as well as some creative ideas with fresh fruit.

The Crown is a lovely place to have a full-blown special vegetarian meal.

Open: 12.30-2, 7.30-9.45 daily (3-5 afternoon tea — only
    Saturday and Sunday in winter)
Restaurant 27, parlour 22, Bar 38 seats
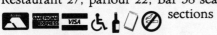 sections

Eat Naturally and Spirals

11 Wensum Street, Norwich, NR3 1LA
☎ 0603 660838
🏠 Eat Naturally £6 day, £9 evening, Spirals £3

Here is a straightforward wholefood and vegetarian restaurant, 'vegans welcome', serving straightforward food. It is informal with round, cloth-covered tables, and a small bar. The meals are good value, and constant changes to the menus means that the food is not repetitive.

Lunch-time food is fairly plain, with the more elaborate fare being served in the evening. Starters might be pears in Stilton sauce or garlic mushrooms. We had a raised pie as a main course, filled with nuts and mushrooms. The filling was tasty and very moist, surrounded by a very nutty pastry. The fresh pasta that came with pesto was also good. Other choices included a cheese and vegetable cobbler, and a filo pie stuffed with feta cheese.

Puddings include an unusual Castlefruit Pudding, which was great, boozy trifle, which certainly lived up to its name, and cheesecake.

The wine list is excellent, much being supplied from local merchants, and the house wine is well worth drinking.

Below Eat Naturally, and run by the same team, is Spirals. This, as the name would imply, is mainly a pasta place, but you can also get pizzas and pancakes. It is rather cave-like with a bistro atmosphere, which appeals to younger people and those with little money to eat out as all the dishes are under £3.

Overall, the feeling on both floors is friendly and unhurried. There is a commitment here to vegetarianism, but there is no proselytising and certainly no boring food.

Open:10-3, 6-10.30 Monday-Saturday
60 seats
 section

The King's Pantry

9 Kings Parade, Cambridge, CB2 1SJ
☎ 0223 321551
 £4

Just opposite Kings chapel, this small basement restaurant is
prevented from being dreary with its whitewashed walls, floral
tablecloths and staff in wholesome green!

They serve a good range of daily specials, such as potato and
apple bake, spinach and cheese tagliatelli, or bulgur wheat and
mushroom bake. Some dishes are better than others. The Padan
e Fagioli was good, whilst the Taco was rather disappointing.
The salad platters are generous and all fairly reliable, if not
terribly exciting.

There is a good choice of tasty puddings and cakes. Some
thoughtful touches, such as jugs of water on the tables, make
you feel someone takes care of the place. Friendly and informal,
King's Pantry is good for a wholesome lunch or a casual meal in
the evening.

Open: 9-5.30 daily, 7-9.30 Wednesday-Saturday
40 seats

Lovetts

142 High Street, Epping, Essex, CM16 4AG
 0378 73960
£9

This is a fairly pleasant wine bar cum restaurant with its soft lighting, hanging dried plants and colour co-ordinated table decorations — though the overall effect is a little bland.

The food is good, though there is nothing particularly memorable. Traditional starters, such as soup, avocado and deep-fried mushrooms are on the menu and the main courses are nut roast, stir-fry or lasagne.

The prices are reasonable, but extras in the form of side-orders tend to make the bill add up.

Open:7.30-10.30 Tuesday-Saturday
26 seats

Mary's Tea Rooms

Walberswick, Nr Southwold, IP18 6UG
☎ 0502 723243
 £7 day £11 evening

This is a small country restaurant that, rather unexpectedly,
provides good vegetarian food. There is always one dish on the
menu and several suitable starters and puddings. The owners
use products grown locally to their best advantage. Great care is
taken with the cooking, even though the dishes themselves are
fairly simple
   Starters include good old standbys, such as spiced grapefruit,
and egg mayonnaise. Main courses include lentil croquettes with
parsley sauce, nut roast with a tomato and garlic relish, Red
Dragon Pie and almond risotto.
   For pudding there is Bakewell tart, profiteroles, ice-creams and
so on.
   In the evening there is a set menu of three courses (plus
coffee) featuring more elaborate food. You do need to book for
these meals in advance.
   The dining room walls of this restaurant are quite a feature.
They are bedecked (an appropriate word) with a marvellous
seascape of flotsam and jetsam, bits of ship wrecks, fishing nets
and floats, and sailors' memorabilia. It really is most imaginative
and original.

Open: 10-6 Tuesday-Thursday and Sunday, 7.15-9 Friday and
      Saturday in Summer, Friday, Saturday and Sunday
      November-March, closed all January.
Credit cards: none
45 seats
♿ 🍴 🗋 🚭

The Mecca

5 Orford Hill, Norwich, NR1 3QB
☎ 0603 760528
 £4

The Mecca is in the centre of Norwich above Taylors, a well-known and well-stocked delicatessen. It is a purely vegetarian and wholefood restaurant, popular with 'conventional' eaters, families and many older people. The surroundings are elegant, with pink and white table-cloths on round tables. The service is calm and courteous.

   The food is nothing out of the ordinary in terms of content, but is tasty and well prepared. The starters are soup or mushroom pâté and the main courses include hazelnut roast and aubergine burgers. We tried the cauliflower pie, which was delicious, with very good wholemeal pastry, but the accompanying side-salad was unexceptional. There are good wholefood cakes, such as carob and carrot, as well as less wholesome meringues for sweet afters.

Open:8.30-5.30 Monday to Saturday
Credit cards: none
40 seats

🍾 📖 🚭

The Ostrich Inn

Stocks Green, Castle Acre, King's Lynn, Norfolk, PE32 2AE
☎ 07605 398
🏠 £4

The Ostrich Inn is a beautiful sixteenth-century coaching inn, complete with exposed beams, wooden interior and open fire places. The setting is lovely — not only does the pub have a large garden, but it is surrounded by pretty countryside with plenty of possibilities for walking, and Castle Acre, as you might guess, has a castle too.

The head chef here used to own a wholefood and vegetarian business that was so successful that it grew too big and demanding. He then took the job here and has already expanded the vegetarian menu.

There are usually two or three choices that are a far cry from the ubiquitous lasagne and Stroganov. When we visited there was a chilli chick pea casserole with saffron rice, or a brazil nut and bulgur wheat burger, served with a mixed salad and orange dressing. More usual items also feature on the menu, such as pizzas, which looked very good, ploughman's lunches and, dare I mention them, omelettes. The bread and cakes for sale are made by a local bakery.

The prices were reasonable and the portions just right. Other tea rooms and restaurants in the area were much more expensive and certainly couldn't offer you a decent wholefood meal.

Hopefully, The Ostrich Inn will go on increasing the menu, though not so much that the chef feels he needs to move on again!

Open: 12-2, 7.30-10.30 Monday-Saturday, 12-1.30, 7.30-10.00
       Sunday
Credit cards: none
60 seats
♿ 🍾 📝 🚭

The Queen's Head

Blyford, Halesworth, Suffolk, IP19 9JY
☎ 0502 70 404
🏠 £6

This thatched, country pub, opposite Blyford church, is in a beautiful setting with a good garden for sitting out and eating in during the summer. There is a jolly, friendly atmosphere with efficient service and very helpful owners. They made special pitta bread for the children in our party, arranged by a phoning up in advance.

Some of the dishes served have lovely, unusual touches. We tried baked feta as a starter. The warm chunks of cheese were served on wholemeal bread and with salad. I thought this idea worked very well. The salads too were imaginative: four types of lettuce, pine nuts and olives with a liberal sprinkling of cold pressed olive oil. There were also stuffed mushrooms, humus and a fresh spinach and lentil soup. Savouries included warm onion quiche and asparagus tart. The cheese and potato pie we had was made of a crisp pastry shell, filled with a moist potato mixture and served with perfectly cooked vegetables. It was flavoursome and sustaining as well as being beautifully presented. Puddings, too, were somewhat more than the run-of-the-mill apple pie and so on. There was a gorgeous greengage fool, a strawberry meringue and a walnut and maple tart.

This pub is making a great effort, and succeeding in producing simple but high-quality vegetarian food. The non-veggie stuff looked pretty good too!

Open:12-2, 7-10 daily
Credit cards: none
40 seats, plus garden

Rebecca's

42 St Mary's Street, Bungay, Norfolk, NR35 1AX
☎ 0986 4691
🏠 £4

This charming restaurant is housed in an old double-fronted shop that, in days gone by, was a bakery. The interior is light and smart with a plain wooden floor and pale grey paintwork. It is tasteful, yet easy and welcoming, making this a splendid place to go for a casual lunch or a more gourmet treat on a Saturday evening.

Attention is very personal as Rebecca's is run by a husband and wife team — she cooks and he waits on tables. All the vegetarian food is highly recommended. The soups are always tasty, often rather light with good flavours. There is usually a choice such as cauliflower and lentil, or leek and potato.

There is a huge variety of salads, freshly prepared with lovely mixtures of ingredients. These, when served with decent portions of quiche for under £1 must be one of the culinary bargains of East Anglia.

Other savouries include nut paella, nut roast with orange sauce, and stuffed marrow. The menu changes frequently and a lot will depend on what is in season at the time. Day-time puddings are of the homely type with rhubarb crumble and syrup sponge.

In the evenings there is more choice on the menu and the food is fancier. There are dips, salads and avocado concoctions for starters, with main courses of layered terrine with red wine and tomato sauce, stir-fried vegetables in filo pastry, and ratatouille with a creamy mushroom ring. Puddings are more exotic with hot banana wraps and chocolate truffle cake. The Russian caravan tea is excellent (40p per pot!). Rebecca's is not licensed, but the owners are quite happy for you to bring your own wine if you wish.

Rebecca's has been established only a year or so. It is certainly highly recommended, not only for the food, but for the way in which you are welcomed, whether for a pot of tea or a full-blown meal. It is easy to impress non-veggies here too.

Open:9.30-5.30 Monday-Friday, 7.45-9.30 (last orders)
        Saturday
30 seats

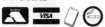

Samphire

3 High Street, Loddon, Norwich, NR14 6ET
☎ 0508 28164
🏠 £5 day £10 evening

Loddon is a large village cum small market town between
Norwich and Lowestoft.

The restaurant has a cool interior, but a welcoming feeling and
is furnished with a mixture of old tables seating between two
and six each.

The cooking at Samphire is cosmopolitan, rich and influenced
by the seasons and availability of good local produce, of which
samphire must be one of the best known.

The day-time food is quite simple, with soup — always
vegetarian and always excellent — pizzas, baked potatoes and
salads. In the evening there is a more extensive menu. Sally's
stuffed mushrooms are a wonderfully rich starter and quite a
meal in themselves — the flavour is superb. There is a most
interesting Brie and grapefruit mousse, and red lentil and cumin
pâté. More soups to try, with some lovely combinations of
vegetables, are sweetcorn and marrow.

There is only one vegetarian main course (if you are phoning
up to book, you can always request an alternative if you don't
like the sound of what is on offer). We've eaten here several
times and the dishes have always been good, served with just
tender fresh vegetables.

There are rich puddings, such as Banoffi (biscuit base with
fudgy bananas and cream), honey and apple cake, chocolate
walnut and toffee tart, sorbets and so on.

It is good to have somewhere that gives you a sense of
occasion for an evening out. There is also a nice bar area here
where you can have a drink before your meal.

Open:9.30-4.30 Monday-Saturday, 7.30-10 Tuesday-Saturday,
    12-2, 7.30-10 Sunday
25 seats

The Tree House

16 Dove Street, Norwich NR2 1DE
☎ 0603 625560
🏠 £5

This busy café-type restaurant, run by a very friendly co-operative, serves good, quality food. The place seems to appeal more to younger people and maybe this is because it is always bright, busy and plenty of fun.

Their soups are always tasty, and often a meal in themselves. The main courses are good, too, though they do tend to vary depending on who is doing the cooking. The style is hearty wholefood with chilli bean casserole, ratatouille and cheese, and spicy curries with raita and dhal. The main courses come with salads, but you can have them separately — there are usually about four salads to choose from with imaginative combinations and some interesting dressings.

The puddings are delicious — sticky peach cake, coffee and walnut fudge slice, or carob and orange gâteau — though often if you have a starter and main course it is hard to find the room to fit one in!

The Tree House is not licensed but you are welcome to bring your own wine.

All the dishes are labelled vegan (V), gluten-free (GF) and sugar-free (SF) where appropriate.

Occasionally there are gourmet evenings at The Tree House. It is essential to book for these, and there is a set menu of three courses for £9.50. The food is more exotic for these evenings with starters such as blue cheese and pecan stuffed pears, and stuffed Gruyère pastry as a main course.

Look out, too, for the occasional cookery courses they run.

Open:11.30-3 Monday-Saturday, occasional gourmet evenings
Credit cards: none
30 seats

North West

Cheshire, Lancashire, Greater Manchester

The Abbey Green Restaurant in Chester gets my award in this region for the best place to eat.

There is quite a good choice over the rest of the region, though many places are more along the lines of the basic veggie variety, and some others are more café-style than restaurant. Generally there is a wholefood emphasis throughout, and a good commitment to vegetarian food from the places that are really more geared up to serve meat and fish.

Apart from the two restaurants mentioned in Manchester, there are a good range of Indian vegetarian restaurants, particularly in Rusholme. Many of these are very cheap, and the cooking is authentic. In the city, the Royal Exchange and several of the galleries also have some vegetarian choices.

Liverpool is well served with places to get vegetarian food and there's a good choice of style and price. The places I've reviewed are round the city centre, but it's also worth visiting Lark Lane towards Aigburth Vale for some trendy wine bars and ethnic eating places.

The Abbey Green Restaurant ✓

2 Abbey Green, Northgate Street, Chester, Cheshire, CH1 2JH
☎ 0244 313251
£5 day £12 evening

This delightful restaurant is about five minutes from the centre of Chester, down a little cobbled street in a Georgian House.

They make every effort to please you, whether you are dropping in for a bite at lunch-time or going to indulge in the gourmet menu in the evening, complete with classical music and rosy pink lighting. After your meal there's a chance to curl up on a sofa in the little coffee lounge and maybe do a spot of entertaining the other guests by playing the piano provided!

The menus for lunch and evening at Abbey Green are different, but all the food on offer is well prepared and well presented.

The day-time food is quite cheap, and sustaining. There is always a soup, pâté, such as carrot and apricot, falafels, or jacket potatoes if you want a light meal. More substantial is the hot dish, such as cheese and leek pie, which comes with salad, or potato and salad garnish. There are herbal teas and a variety of fresh juices on offer, and a good range of home baking.

In the evening the menu is richer and more elaborate, and you are encouraged to spoil yourself and relax as you wine and dine. The starters could be asparagus in filo pastry, or cucumber and mint cheesecake. The main courses comprise Peking vegetables with spicy saté sauce, or chestnut and mushroom loaf *en croûte*.

There is a good selection of sweets and they have a substantial wine list with a good choice of organic varieties.

Apart from enjoying the food, there's plenty to look at as you eat as they offer gallery space to local artists. Worth a visit at any time, whether you're looking for a wholesome lunch or a very special night out.

Open: 11.30-2.30 Monday, 11.30-2.30, 6.30-9.45 (last orders)
      Tuesday-Saturday
50 seats

Armadillo Restaurant

20 Mathew Street, Liverpool, L2 6RE
☎ 051-236 4123
🏠 £7 day £10 evening

In my student days in Liverpool I remember the whole area
around the Armadillo being pretty run down, and the original
café had somewhat the same feeling. Over the last few years
there has been considerable redevelopment, and this restaurant,
too, has certainly smartened up. There's a 'Habitat' feel to the
decor with the polished parquet floor, pine chairs and royal blue
table-cloths.

The menu is not entirely vegetarian, but there are always at
least two suitable starters and two main courses, and they make
an effort to cater for vegans too. We had stuffed peppers with a
tomato sauce. These were well prepared, and more interesting
than the average stuffed pepper because each one had a different
filling — one of lentils, nuts and mushrooms, and the other of
bulgur, spinach and cheese. Also on the menu were mushrooms
with dill and blinis, and a couple of quiches.

The main-course dishes are served with hot vegetables or
salads, and the choice is really good — at least eight or nine
interesting, fresh mixtures. The menu remains similar for the
early supper period and then, in the evenings, the food is a little
more elaborate and expensive, and, if anything, there is slightly
less choice, though as a vegetarian, you will still have a very
pleasant evening out.

Open: 12-3 Monday, 12-3, 5-7 Tuesday and Wednesday,
        7.30-10 Thursday and Friday, 7.30-11.30 Saturday
Credit cards: none
80 seats

As You Like It

51 Promenade, Southport, Merseyside, PR9 0DX
☎ 0704 35886
 £6

As You Like It is on the ground floor of a private hotel, just off
the sea front at Southport. The building is Victorian and the
entrance to the restaurant rather grand. The rooms are spacious
too and the decor in keeping with the period with Victorian-style
wallpaper and dado rail.

The sense of eating in what must once have been a splendid
room adds to the atmosphere, but the friendly approach of the
staff keeps the place very informal.

The menu includes an enormous range of vegetarian savouries
and wholefood cakes and puddings. Most items are on display
in a large counter. You can gaze to your heart's delight before
ordering and they do explain anything you can't recognize. After
you order the food is brought over to the table.

Typical starters might be coriander and carrot soup, humus
and roll, or cottage cheese and cashew pâté. The main courses
are quite basic, but tasty, well presented and the portions
generous. There are lots of 'layer'-type bakes — lasagne,
moussaka, and *gratins* — plus nut loaf and vegeburgers.

Puddings range from the rich — chocolate mousse — to the
rib-sticking — bread-and-butter pudding. There are plenty of
drinks of both the alcoholic and non-alcoholic variety to wash it
down.

As You Like It is a good stop-off point for a light snack lunch
if you are on route to the beach or venue for a casual night out.

Open: 10.30-10.30 Tuesday-Sunday
Credit cards: none
50 seats

🍾 📋 🚭

Burnley Mechanics Arts and Entertainment Centre

Manchester Road, Burnley, Lancashire, BB11 1JA
☎ 0282 30055
 £4

This is a thriving community arts centre with regular events in the theatre (professional and amateur), plus courses and craft workshops for adults and children.

The coffee shop and bar was done up about two years ago and still looks smart. There is a thirties feel — lots of mahogany and glass, with interesting artifacts from the mills.

There is at the moment only one choice on the menu for vegetarians, very much on the lines of quiche or cauliflower cheese, but The Burnley Mechanics deserves a place in this guide for its pleasant, friendly atmosphere and cultural activities.

Open: 12-2 daily
Credit cards: none
Coffee shop 25, Shuttle bar 60 seats

& ♭ ▱ ◑

Carrageen Café

9 Myrtle Parade, Myrtle Street, Liverpool, L7 7EL
☎ 051-727 5021
🏠 £4

The food at Carrageen is good, clean, simple and nicely served.
Everything is made in the kitchen at the back of the small
counter where you go to order your food.

  Hot dishes, such as cheese and potato pie, which was very
tasty, are reheated in the microwave. The menu is not vast and,
apart from the special of the day, includes soup, pasties, quiche
and salads. The prices are very cheap and the portions good.

  The surroundings though are to be borne rather than enjoyed.
The walls are covered with posters about various events and the
tables are arranged in fours, sixes and eights, so at busy times
you will have to share with the regular clientele. The area
around the café is rough. Lots of the shops have shutters or
grills on the windows and, although parking is available, ensure
your car is locked. Overall, however, while being nothing
special, Carrageen makes a useful place for a wholesome lunch
or snack.

Open: 12-6.30 Monday-Friday, 12-4 Saturday
Credit cards: none
40 seats
&. 🍽 🚭

Coconut Willy's

37 St Petersgate, Stockport, Cheshire, SK1 1DH
☎ 061-480 7013
🏠 £8

Coconut Willy's offers a wide range of cuisines for both its evening meal service and the slightly snackier style day-time menu. You might get spicy Indian meals, Greek dishes, or Japanese hors-d'oeuvres! There are starters such as tofu dip or humus and a good choice of salads is displayed — maybe up to eight at a busy time. There are home-made quiches and pizzas, as well as a good selection of cakes. If you don't want a full-blown meal in the day, you can just have a baked potato with filling.

Your food can be washed down with a good selection of organic wines and beers.

This versatile restaurant has a pleasant, friendly atmosphere, pleasant for light, day-time eating, and, with the dimmed lights, a cosy place for a casual evening meal.

Open: 11.30-10 Tuesday-Saturday
40 seats
VISA 🍾 📓 🚭 section

The Duke's Restaurant

The Duke's Theatre, Moor Lane, Lancaster, LA1 1QE
☎ 0524 67461
 £4

Recently redecorated in pastel colours with delicate pink walls and pale blue and white tablecloths, The Duke's Restaurant, part of the Duke's Theatre, is a very pleasant place to eat. The food, too, is pleasant without being in any way particularly special. Starters consist of a good soup served with wholemeal bread, melon platter and stuffed tomatoes. For the main course, there was cannelloni and salad, or paella, which was rather disappointing as it consisted of little more than rice with a few vegetables, the odd raisin and piece of walnut. The salad was a simple mixture of lettuce, tomatoes etc, but was crisp and very fresh. To follow there was an apricot flan, which was delicious, and a slightly dry apple pie. We had coffee after that, which came with plenty of chocolates!

As a place that is really catering for meat-eaters, the vegetarian choice is reasonable. They are certainly keen to please and would probably welcome suggestions to make the menu more imaginative in time. Full marks though for the theatre restaurant where it is possible to have some choice, as many such places fail miserably when it comes to vegetarian fare.

Open: 10-2.30 Monday-Saturday, 6-9.30 Tuesday-Saturday
Credit cards: none
34 seats

🍾 ⬜ 🍽

Everyman Bistro

9-11 Hope Street, Liverpool, L1 9BH
☎ 051-708 9545
📞 £5

The basement bistro at the Everyman Theatre has long been established as a place to get good food. Years ago when I was a student in Liverpool, I thought it was *the* place to haunt.

The atmosphere is lively and the style of eating casual, with counter service that you queue for, often having to create your own space. It is not all that comfortable as the seating is arranged round long, wooden tables. Those seated in the middle invariably have to clamber in, and often you'll have to share. There's no hassle here, though — you can take your time over the food and drink. There's plenty to look at, both on the walls, and in the form of other clientele.

The vegetarian choice is reasonable. The menu, as you would expect from the surroundings, lists basic, substantial food. Soup, humus and roll or jacket potatoes with various fillings and pizza are the lighter meals available, with vegetable *gratin*, vegetable curry and rice, or spinach roulade and salad as the main courses. These change frequently. There are also salads, sold by the portion or as a mixed bowl. Once you have chosen your food, anything hot is plated up and then microwaved. This makes the service a little slow when the place is busy, which it often is.

There is a good choice of cakes and gâteaux, coffee, tea and so on, and a choice of alcoholic drinks served at the bar, which is separate.

Open: 12-10.30 Monday-Thursday, 12-12 Friday and Saturday,
        12-10.30 Sunday
Credit cards: none
100 seats

The Greenhouse   ✓

331 Great Western Street, Rusholme, Manchester, M14 4AN
☎ 061-224 0730
▯ £8

Transport cafe, snack bar, café and restaurant all combine together in The Greenhouse, which offers all sorts of meals, day and evening, at very good prices.

For breakfast, you can have a near-traditional fry-up of sausage (vegetarian, of course), beans, potato cake and mushrooms, plus tea and toast for under £2. Or how about starting the day the eastern way with a meal of humus, pitta, yoghurt, olives and fruit.

These ideas, classed as light snacks, believe it or not, are served from 10-5, as well as burgers, cheese on toast, pizza, and spring rolls. Burgers and sandwiches are sold to take away as well.

I've eaten the more conventional fare at The Greenhouse at both lunch-times and in the evenings. Generally it has been very good, though, as with many of these places, the menu makes a dish sound more tempting than it is.

I had a delicious starter of Japanese oyster mushrooms in red wine. Other starters include Boursinette — a dip made from soft cheese — or samosas. The main courses include moussaka, hazelnut and brown rice roast, stuffed vegetables or chilli, served with vegetables and salads and are quite substantial. The Greenhouse strudel deserves a special mention. It is a tasty filo pastry roll, filled with two sauces, one of creamy mushroom and one of spinach. About half the menu is vegan and it changes quarterly.

Puddings are varied. How about a vegan Knickerbocker Greenhouse? Also on offer are rum babas and apple strudel. I adore fruit crumble and struggled through one of the largest, but most irresistible, portions here. There is also plenty of choice in the way of beverages of both the alcoholic and non-alcoholic varieties.

Rumour had it that the place may change hands. If this is true, I hope any new owners are able to carry on the good work.

Open: 10-11 Monday-Friday, 6-11 Saturday, 1-11 Sunday
Credit cards: none
38 seats

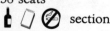 section

Greens ✓

43 Lapwing Lane, West Didsbury, Manchester, M20 8NT
☎ 061-434 4259
 £6

This pleasant, homely restaurant is furnished with a marvellously eclectic collection of furniture and ornaments. This gives the place a friendly, casual feeling.

The menu here changes daily, though the basic format remains the same, with starters such as soup and pâté.

The main courses are quite simple. There is usually a nut roast and then choices such as vegetable crumble, stuffed courgettes, or aubergine galette. These are accompanied by a good green salad.

For pudding there are various cakes and a fruit salad, which will vary considerably. We had a delicious mixture of kiwi fruit with ginger.

Greens is a good place to eat. The food is well prepared and reasonably priced. It is advisable to book, especially at weekends.

Open: 10-5 Tuesday, 10-9.30 Wednesday-Saturday
Credit cards: none
32 seats

Libra

19 Brock Street, Lancaster, LA1 1UR
☎ 0524 61551
 £3

This is a small, clean café offering simple, wholesome fare, much of it for under £2. The menu is limited with a few starters, such as soup, humus, egg mayonnaise and pâté, followed by pie, quiche or a nut meat roll. The fillings of the pie and quiche vary daily according to what is in season. Other popular dishes include a spiced potato dish, alu koftas, samosas and some tiny, individual pizzas. There are some good salads to choose from and some wholemeal cakes and puddings. The range of drinks is extensive with herbal teas, coffee and coffee substitutes, plus alcoholic and non-alcoholic drinks.

Libra has recently decided to add one late night (Friday) to its schedule. They tried changing the menu for the evening, but found that the customers preferred to eat the same dishes they served during the day. A useful place for lunch while you are out in town, or for a bite before the pictures or theatre.

Open: 9-6 Monday-Saturday, 9-10 Friday
Credit cards: none
30 seats

🍾 🍽 🚭

The Nutcracker

43 Oxford Road, Altrincham, Cheshire, WA14 2ED
☎ 061-928 4399
🏠 £5

This is a large restaurant, typical in decor, with its stripped-pine look, wooden tables and plenty of plants. At the far end is the large serving counter.

The menu follows a fairly standard format with soups, specials and so on. The specials are written on a small board and most of the rest of the food is on display under glass. There are usually two types of soup with some unusual combinations, such as carrot, apple and cashew. Recently the main courses have also become more adventurous. Zyldyke is a popular Dutch dish of mixed vegetables in a mild sauce, but you may find lentil and chick pea passandra, which is a spicy, curry mixture with bananas. There are also quiches and pizza slices. Do try some of the salads at the Nutcracker — I've always been impressed with the range available and the imaginative mixtures, even though the portions are sometimes on the small side (a lot depends, though, on when you go and what is left). They offer a choice of three or of six for roughly double the price. All the cheese used is vegetarian and the eggs are free range, plus other organic ingredients as and when they are available.

Cakes and puddings are much in evidence, quite a few using chocolate, but many are made with wholemeal flour. They also have a good range of drinks, including an additive-free, low-sugar lemonade.

The restaurant is clean and neat. The service is fairly friendly, though sometimes a little slow as there is quite a lot of dishing up of salads and calling through to the kitchen for orders. The Nutcracker is a good place for a tasty lunch or for light snacks through the day.

Open: 10-4.45 Monday-Saturday (close 2pm Wednesday)
Credit cards: none
60 seats
 section

On The Eighth Day Co-op Ltd. ✓

111 Oxford Road, All Saints, Manchester, M1 7DU
☎ 061-273 1850
🏠 £3

Established now for several years, this co-operative still offers solid, rib-sticking fare at extremely low prices. On The Eighth Day is very popular with the students at the nearby university and many other regulars from the surrounding offices, including a few people from the BBC studios!

The restaurant is a large, squarish room, sparsely furnished with a variety of wooden tables. There is the predictable plethora of useful notices. It is useful that they are open in the early evenings for anyone not wanting to have to bother with supper once they get home.

The menu is very basic and unpretentious. There is always on offer some type of soup, casserole and bake, and they simply try to vary the ingredients so that the three are at least different from each other. The soup and casserole are usually vegan and are kept warm in vast pots behind the counter. There is one salad mixture available, and you can choose either a small or large portion.

Some puddings and cakes are available and these are often vegan too. There is a range of hot and cold drinks, but, as they are not licensed, you cannot buy a glass or bottle of wine to go with your meal. However, you are welcome to bring your own if you wish.

The food served here doesn't change the 'beans and lentils' image of vegetarianism as it is all solid, substantial and rather piled on the plate, but that has never been a priority in this particular restaurant. They are more concerned that the food is cheap and filling, which they certainly manage to achieve. For fancier gourmet vegetarian food, go elsewhere. They do, however, try to make the most of seasonal foods and alter the menu to do this. The odd gourmet cake has crept in recently, too, such as Drambuie gâteau, or coffee and walnut cake (these are not made on the premises but bought in). On The Eighth Day, therefore, is perfect if you are used to wholefoods and you simply want a basic meal.

Open: 10-7 Monday-Friday, 10-4.30 Saturday
Credit cards: none
43 seats
🍴◯| 🚭

Rumours Bistro

148 Congleton Road, Sandbach, Cheshire, CW11 0DG
☎ 0270 763664
£6

Fast efficient service, traditional pub decor and an informal
atmosphere make Rumours a pleasant, homely place to eat. The
early opening time in the evening is useful if you are looking for
a family meal and have young children.

There are usually six vegetarian dishes available and these
change frequently. The snag is that they may all contain cheese,
though vegans could rough it on the salad and potatoes as these
were certainly good enough to make a meal on their own.
Starters consist of mushroom fritters or egg mayonnaise, but you
can order side-dishes instead, such as herb bread or stir-fried
vegetables. The main courses may include pizza, bhajis,
aubergine and cheese fritters or vegetables in a cheese sauce.
What is on the menu is written up on the blackboard and you
order before sitting down.

Open: 12-2, 6-10.15 (last orders) daily
50 seats

Top Table

11 Brown Street, Burnley, Lancashire, BB11 1PJ
☎ 0282 416732
🏠 £3

This is a pleasant little café in the town centre with plenty of parking nearby.

There are two main courses for vegetarians. We tried the mushroom soup, which was very tasty and served with a good brown herb bread. We also had a good vegetable goulash with hot garlic bread. There was a spiced lentil quiche available, and jacket potatoes and salads.

The food is largely prepared while you wait. Having chosen your food at the counter, it is brought fairly quickly to your table. The staff were cheerful and friendly, the atmosphere homely and clean. Top Table is a good place for a wholesome lunch if you are passing.

Open: 9-5 Monday-Saturday, closes at 2 Tuesday
Credit cards: none
40 seats

📙 🚭 section

Veggies

Tarleton Street, Liverpool
☎ none
🏠 £3

Veggies is a small, central Liverpudlian café. It has a cafeteria-style interior with formica-topped tables, seating two or four, and some built-in pine benches. The surroundings are clean but the loos are primitive!

The menu is very basic, featuring mainly snack-type food. Soup, vegeburgers, quiche and schnitzel are the savouries on offer, plus filled or plain jacket potatoes. There are some filled rolls, cakes, caramel bars, tea and coffee. By the door is a counter for take-aways.

Veggies is useful as a pit stop rather than as a venue for a special outing.

Open: 9.30-4.30 Monday-Saturday
Credit cards: none
44 seats

Woody's

5 King Street, Delph, Saddleworth, OL3 5DL
☎ 04577 71197
🏠 £4 day £9 evening

Although Woody's was only opened in the summer of 1988, it
has already established an excellent reputation, and it is
certainly advisable to book.

The place is very small, but nicely furnished in a Victorian
style, with comfortable seating, lace tablecloths and cut glass.
All these touches are designed to get away from the typical
scrubbed pine usually associated with vegetarian restaurants.

At lunch-time it is possible to order light meals and snacks,
such as chilli, burgers, quiche and à special Woody's pie. In the
evening though, it's worth taking time over your meal.

The menu changes every three months and there are several
starters, such as potted port and Wensleydale, tangy avocado,
hot melon salad and vichyssoise. Main courses cover a range of
cuisines, from rogan josh to neapolitan peppers, so there is
something to suit everyone. There are usually five choices and
these are served with either potato and hot vegetables or salad.

Do save room for the rich brandy and chocolate mousse cake,
or meringue Chantilly, to name but two of the rich puddings.
The wine list includes some organic varieties.

Woody's is a welcome newcomer to the vegetarian scene and,
hopefully, will stay the course.

Open: 12-2, 7.30-11 Tuesday-Friday, 12-3, 7.30-11 Saturday
      and Sunday
20 seats

Yorkshire and Humberside

North, South and West Yorkshire, Humberside

There are a variety of tourist centres in this region, most of which have some vegetarian food on offer.

The best, perhaps, is York where you can get the cheap and cheerful variety at The Bees Knees, as well as delicious meals in sophisticated surroundings at Oat Cuisine.

Whitby has a delightful café cum restaurant, which is linked to an excellent wholefood shop. I was also delighted to find a pleasant little basement coffee house in the dignified Victorian spa town of Harrogate.

The more industrial centres of Leeds, Bradford and Hull are sadly lacking in places to recommend, though you will certainly find pizzas and curries. Sheffield has a little more to offer, which is encouraging, including good food at the Crucible Theatre, a trend that would be welcomed by theatre-goers everywhere.

The Bay Tree

119 Devonshire Street, Sheffield, S3 7SB
☎ 0742 759254
🏠 £6 day, £10 evening

Apart from one fish dish, the food at The Bay Tree is vegetarian and it is very good.

The menu is chalked up on a blackboard and changes weekly. There is always a soup to start and several main courses to choose from, such as crispy mushroom layer, cashew nut loaf, stuffed aubergines or vegetable crumble. All come served with an excellent salad, full of all the usual salad ingredients plus cracked wheat, rice and a variety of beans.

There are various cakes to finish off the meal, such as pecan slice or banana cake.

The restaurant has a nice, homely feel, and the staff are very friendly and efficient. It is popular, so not the place for a romantic tête-à-tête, but, as the space is divided up into four small rooms, you can feel a little more private when it is not so busy. Be early to get the best choice as lunch is served from 12 noon, and when it is all gone, that's it. Overall it is easy to feel comfortable and relaxed here.

On Fridays, they are open in the evening too, but, it is essential to book. There is table service and a three-course meal will cost you £9.50.

Open: 10-4 Monday-Saturday, 7-11 Friday
Credit cards: none
48 seats

The Bees Knees

Millers Yard, Gillygate, York, North Yorkshire YO3 7EB
☎ 0904 610676
🏠 £4

I learned how to bake at the Gillygate bakery when it was in tiny premises over the road from the present site. They wanted to expand then to a café, and rightly so as they were doing the most tremendous range of cakes, pasties and savoury breads. The new premises made this possible. The set up is a bakery shop and small café combined.

The menu is straightforward, offering standard fare such as soup, a selection of salads, quiches, savouries and perhaps two main hot dishes each day. There are, of course, all the old favourites such as pasties and pizzas. They make an effort to cater for vegans.

The Bees Knees pride themselves on the enormous range of teas they offer, as well as soft drinks and, although they are not licensed, you are welcome to bring your own wine if you want to.

Opening times may vary from winter to summer, so it's best to check. In the summer too they have seating in the garden. This is a good place for a casual lunch-time meal or snack, and a chance to replenish the bread bin!

Open: 10-4 Monday-Saturday
Credit cards: none
30 seats + garden seating

Bonnet's

38 Huntress Row, Scarborough, North Yorkshire, YO11 2EF
☎ 0723 361033
🏠 £3

Bonnet's was a favourite haunt in my Scarborough days. Then it specialized in hand-made chocolates. Now, in addition to this business, there is a delightful, comfortable café that caters quite well for vegetarians.

In keeping with the traditions of the shop, the café is beautifully furnished in a Victorian style with William Morris wallpaper, plush, dark blue carpet, mahogany tables and wicker chairs. On the walls there are pictures of the chocolate-making process, and old photographs showing the history of Bonnet's since it started in the late 1800s.

The specialities of the house, naturally, are the confectionary and pâtisserie, all made without animal fat and gelatine, so you can indulge to your heart's content! You can choose from chocolate cake, cheesecake, home-made lemon curd meringue, and many others.

On the savoury side, there is usually a suitable soup, though always check as to whether it is vegetarian or not, and a choice of quiches, baked potatoes with various fillings, stuffed pancakes and a good selection of salads.

The owners, John and Anne, are always full of new ideas. They plan to open a smart restaurant upstairs during the summer of 1989. This will be in addition to the present café, and should certainly be worth a visit.

Open: 9.30-5.15 Monday-Saturday
65 seats

Cookes

661 London Road, Sheffield, S2 4HT
 0742 550545
£9

Cookes is about a mile south of the Sheffield ring road in the direction of Chesterfield. Its out-of-town location makes it a good spot for an intimate mid-week evening meal as it is less busy then. At weekends you are advised to book.

This is a pretty restaurant, furnished with lots of plants and a collection of unusual biscuit tins of all shapes and sizes. There is pleasant music, low lighting and candles, which all add to the atmosphere. The service is both friendly and efficient.

The menu, which caters for both vegetarians and meat-eaters has some unusual ideas, making the vegetarian options very attractive. We started with cheese 'pies' — tasty puff pastry parcels, filled with cheese and served with plum chutney and salad. There was also soup, corn pancakes and mushrooms in garlic butter.

The aubergine bake main course was delicious. It consisted of layers of cheese and aubergine with an olive and tomato sauce. It was served with an excellent selection of vegetables.

For dessert there were sorbets and sweet pancakes as well as carrot cake (with Grand Marnier!) and strawberry malikoff.

Herbal teas as well as coffee were available to round the meal off.

The menu changes about every three months.

Open: 7-10 Monday-Thursday, til 10.30 Friday-Saturday, 12-3
       Sunday
Credit cards: none
45 seats

Crucible Theatre Restaurant

55 Norfolk Street, Sheffield S1 1DA
☎ 0742 750724
█ £7

This restaurant is an integral part of the modern theatre complex.

There is a set menu with a couple of choices for starters for vegetarians — garlic mushrooms and vegetable pâté. Then a small section of main-course vegetarian dishes, all of a fairly predictable nature, such as lasagne, moussaka and nut roast. The lunch-time selection also includes a grapefruit cocktail and quiche with jacket potato.

The food is quite tasty — our nut roast was good with a very rich sauce.

The restaurant is rather formal with uniformed staff, table service and so on, so is not the sort place to nip into for a coffee, but it is good for a pre-performance meal. If it is a casual snack you need, there is an excellent café upstairs serving soups, pizzas, salads and sandwiches.

Open: Monday-Saturday 11-7
60 seats

 section

The Curlew Café

11-13 Crossgate, Otley, West Yorkshire, LS21 1BD
☎ 0943 464351
🏠 £3 day £8 evening

This small friendly café is just the place to enjoy good
vegetarian food and chat with friends. There is no music, no
hassle and no hurrying or rushing.

In the day-time, light meals are served, such as soup, savoury
flans, omelettes and salads, plus some dishes suitable for
vegans. The range of specials that change throughout the day
are more substantial. There's a good choice of teas, coffees and
coffee substitutes, too, and, although they are not licensed, you
are welcome to bring your own wine if you wish.

They also do a tempting range of cakes and scones. On Friday
and Saturday evenings, there's an international cuisine set
menu. This changes weekly. A Middle-Eastern selection might
consist of ashe mast — a chilled spinach and yoghurt soup —
lentil dip, or falafel, followed by eggah — thick baked omelette
— or harrira — a rich bean stew. Desserts include Turkish fruit
cake and apricot cream. This meal is wonderful value in itself
and, afterwards, you can have unlimited teas and coffee.

Overall, the workers co-operative responsible for running the
Curlew Café make you feel at home and endeavour to look after
you with friendly, efficient service and, above all, good food.

Open: 10.30-4.30 Thursday-Saturday, 7.30-9.30 Friday-
        Saturday international menu, 12-5 Sunday
Credit cards: none
30 seats

Oat Cuisine

13a High Ousegate, York, North Yorkshire, YO1 2RZ
☎ 0904 27929
🏠 £8

I have absolutely no hesitation in recommending this elegant restaurant. My only fear is that it is all too easy to miss! The entrance, advertised with a very subtle sign, is down a tiny alley. Do persevere in your searching — the setting and food here are excellent.

The decor is bold and simple — white, grey and black relieved by a warm-coloured wooden entrance floor and wooden doors inset with thirties-style portholes. There are fresh flowers on the cloth-covered tables, and the soft lighting prevents the place from being too stark. All the furniture is modern and carefully selected pictures adorn the walls.

My first impression was that it would be very expensive, but the prices are reasonable, even though the portions are not huge.

There is a set lunch — ideal for business entertaining — as well as an à la carte section. The menus have been well thought out with a mixture of simple dishes — for example salad platters with cottage cheese, and a ratatouille with French bread — plus some more exotic ideas, such as Jamaican stuffed aubergines. There is also an interesting selection of Mexican specialities. I tried the burritos, which consisted of a very filling, soft, bread-like pancake, stuffed with well-flavoured spinach and cream cheese, and covered with tomato sauce and melted cheese. It was tasty and nicely served. With it was a crisp side-salad made from a good selection of greenery. I had the Oat fruit cocktail for pudding, which was very rich. Served in a tall wine glass, it was a mixture of chopped exotic fruits, smothered in a light cream. Those with bigger appetites could well have tucked into the fruit crumble, or bread-and-butter pudding.

Light meals, such as the layered Oat club sandwich, are also served as well as an excellent range of coffees, mineral waters and freshly pressed juices.

The evening menu repeats some of the same more elaborate main courses, and the starters are more sophisticated. The soup is upgraded to *potage*, served with herb *croùtons*. Mexican dishes feature again, as well as roulades and cannelloni. There are about three or four choices on each course and this menu changes about every six months.

This is a lovely place to have a smart lunch or a splendid special evening out, and would certainly be somewhere to take sceptical carnivores. How I wish we had somewhere as good in my own stamping ground of London!

Although they allow smoking, the staff make an effort to keep smokers' tables together.

Open: 12-5, 7-11 Monday-Saturday
48 seats

The Post House Hotel

Bramhope, Nr Leeds LS16 9JJ
☎ 0532 842911
🛏 £15

The Post House Hotel is a place where you can eat in comfort
and style. The restaurant is very pretty and well furnished, with
a wall of windows overlooking a leafy garden.

There are several starters to choose from, including melon and
mint salad, avocado with yoghurt, or fresh asparagus with
chervil sauce. For a main course we tried the vegetable brochette
served with brown rice and a sharp tomato sauce, which was
very pleasant. There was also available a good fresh pasta dish
— tortellini with a cream and basil sauce. You could also choose
from a variety of salads and they are, of course, willing to make
you an omelette! The menu changes every few months.

It is good that hotels such as this are making more of an effort
to cater imaginatively for vegetarians and I hope more people
choose these options to convince the hotels that it is
worthwhile.

Open: 12.30-2.15, 7-10.15 daily
85 seats

 section

The Shepherd's Purse

95 Church Street, Whitby, North Yorkshire, YO22 4BH
☎ 0947 820228
🏠 £6 day £8 evening

The Shepherd's Purse is part of a complex with a very well
stocked wholefood shop, boutique and dance studio. The
Shepherd's Purse, as a wholefood shop, was established by
Rosie and Pete some 15 years ago, and has deservedly built up
an excellent reputation. The restaurant is only in its third season
and already successful. They are now undertaking more new
projects including offering a limited amount of wholefood B &
B. This attractive restaurant is just off the street, down a small,
cobbled alleyway. The decor is pretty and quite countryfied with
sprigged wallpaper, interesting knick-knackery, beamed ceilings,
dried flowers and a mixture of old tables.

Outside is a small courtyard offering seating in the summer. It
is a very pleasant place to go and certainly very different from
most of the other eating places in Whitby.

The menu is fairly standard with soup, starters such as humus
and side-dishes of garlic bread. Main courses in the day-time
tend to be quite simple casseroles and stir-fries. There are also
quiches, pizzas on Saturday and a mixture of salads.

The evening food is similar, but more elaborate. Time is spent
on presentation so that everything looks most appealing. Extra
ingredients are added to the salads, for example, making them
fancier, and more expensive. Main courses consist of more
complicated dishes, such as moussaka or lasagne.

Good bread is served, and there are always wholefood cakes
and a selection of rich desserts to tempt you.

Open: Seasonal, ring and check

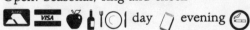 day ⬜ evening ⊜

Toffs Restaurant and Coffee House

23 Matilda Street, The Moor, Sheffield, South Yorkshire,
S1 4QB
☎ 0742 720783
🏠 £4

You can begin with breakfast at Toffs, which is conveniently
situated in a side street just by the main shopping precinct.
Otherwise it is a good place to drop in for coffee or a bite of
lunch if you are in town. The setting is modern with bright
lights, white, wipe-down tables and white plastic chairs.

There is always a soup of the day and several traditional main
courses, such as cauliflower cheese, savoury pancakes and
mixed vegetable quiche. The filling in the quiche was good with
chunky pieces of vegetables and a hint of nutmeg. There are
also salads, rice and potatoes.

Scones, chocolate fudge cake and apple frangipane are offered
for dessert.

Open: 7.30-4 Monday-Saturday
Credit cards: none
45 seats

👤 🍽 🚬

Tubbs

7 Montpelier Parade, Harrogate, North Yorkshire, HG1 2TJ
☎ 0423 508419
🏠 £3

This basement restaurant is pleasantly furnished in a modern
style with blue chairs and white tables, giving it a clean, airy
feel. It is a good place to get snacks rather than full-blown
meals, but I was impressed by the freshness of the food and the
friendly service.

For vegetarians there are several salads to choose from at 75p
per portion. They are reliable rather than special and include
mixed bean, coleslaw, corn and chick pea, cucumber and
yoghurt, and potato. More substantial salad platters consisted of
cottage cheese or egg mayonnaise. Hot choices included
ratatouille, mushrooms à la Grecque, and the trusty baked
potato — well-named in this case 'Tubbspuds'!

Open: 9.30-5 Monday-Saturday
Credit cards: none
50 seats
🗋 🚭 section

Cumbria

There are plenty of restaurants to choose from in Cumbria, many of which are to be found in the central part of the Lake District, such as Ambleside and Grasmere, but there are good eateries elsewhere in this area, particularly further North and East. I was impressed by the variety of places serving good vegetarian food. In fact, I felt that overall there was a particularly high standard in this area, whether it was from the specialist vegetarian restaurants or those that have both meat and non-meat menus.

It is easy to find a wide range of types of meal, from wholesome snacks and light lunches, as well as excellent pub food (and drink), to places to go for a special occasion meal out.

Some of the places reviewed do get very crowded at the height of the season, but there are some mentioned that, by virtue of being slightly more off the beaten track, are less crowded all year round. It is hard to pick a favourite out of such a good bunch, but The Quince and Medlar is my first choice, closely followed by The Village Bakery in Melmerby.

Chesters

Kirkstone Gallery, Skelwith Bridge, Ambleside, LA22 9NN
☎ 05394 33296
🏠 £3

Chesters is not so much a restaurant — more a good place for a hearty afternoon tea in very pleasant, spacious surroundings with parking just outside the door. They offer a variety of teas, including a Lakeland special, and a good cup of coffee (no decaffeinated).

Plenty of wholefood slices and sticky cakes are available, including date slice, marmalade cake and caraway seed cake, but if you have really done some trekking you might be able to manage the more substantial sticky toffee pudding. Just to be on the safe side, ask about the ingredients — the staff are willing to be helpful.

Anyone not wanting instant calories might prefer the savoury main course. There is always a hot dish served at lunch-time, which might be leek gratin, vegetable crumble, tortellini or lasagne. Occasionally the soup is vegetarian and there are salads too, but nothing very imaginative.

The restaurant itself is in the centre of the gallery, and there are some inexpensive and interesting gifts on sale. You'll find the gallery between Ambleside and Coniston on the A593.

Open: 10.15-5.30 daily
Credit cards: none
32 seats

The Drunken Duck Inn

Barngates, Ambleside, Cumbria, LA22 0NG
☎ 09666 347
🏠 £3

I used to have yearly holidays at a farm just close by The Drunken Duck when I was little. I was more than glad to find that this pub is gaining a reputation for its vegetarian food as well as its ale, but try to ignore the hunting trophies if you feel sensitive.

It is popular and gets crowded, so try to get there early to get a full choice — it seems that the vegetarian food runs out first too! We had plenty of choice mid-week at about 7pm, but on Saturday night, going with a party at about 8pm, the vegetarian menu was sadly depleted. However, as it's the sort of place that is sensitive to demand they should start to cook more.

Hot dishes vary. I tried a risotto, which was quite sweetly spiced, and sampled the chilli, which was good. Also on offer were lasagne, cheesy bean bake or stuffed cabbage. One small gripe, they are not very willing to make changes to the dishes. I tried to get them to add a potato to one meal I had, but they would only sell it with the meat pie! It is the usual system with pubs — you should order at the bar and then look around for a table.

The Drunken Duck is outside Ambleside, on a quiet crossroad near Tarn How.

Open: 12-2, 6.30-9 for food, pub hours for drink daily
Credit cards: none
100 seats

🍾 📃 🚬

Eden Coffee Shop

St Andrew's Churchyard, Penrith, Cumbria, CA11 7YG
☎ 0768 67955
🏠 £3

This little café is set above a craft shop and gallery just off the
main street of Penrith. It is run by a husband and wife team
who pride themselves on their home baking.

There are good date slices and flapjacks but, sadly for the
purist, it is not all wholefood and many of the other cakes and
scones are made with a mixture of flours. The savoury
vegetarian menu is limited to a choice of cheese and onion pie
or quiche and a hot special of the day. This is likely to be a
dish along the lines of cheese and leek bake, individual
cauliflower cheese or a mediterranean pasta. Although these
choices are not terribly imaginative, everything is home-made
and no frozen vegetables are used.

I found the café clean and although they don't ban smoking
on account of some regulars, it was not encouraged. The service
was quick and friendly, the coffee drinkable. The gallery and
craft shop have some interesting items.

Open: 9.30-4.30 Monday-Saturday, closed Wednesday and
      from January till Easter
Credit cards: none
24 seats

Harvest ✓

Compston Street, Ambleside, Cumbria LA22 9DJ
☎ 05394 33151
🏠 £7

New owners have recently taken over this vegetarian lakeland favourite, but the food served remains of a good standard. It's all wholesome stuff with some extra touches to make it special. For example, the humus comes with pitta bread and the marinated mushrooms with a side salad, there is a good-value plate of quiche and salad and the baked potatoes come with a choice of fillings such as ratatouille.

There is always a different hot dish of the day. We had a tasty lentil, cheese and vegetable bake served with salad and, rather surprisingly, and unnecessarily I thought, extra grated cheese on top, making the whole thing a bit heavy. It nearly meant I had no room for the terrific hot toffee pudding!

There are all the usual beverages to be had as well as some imaginative whisked drinks to try, such as rosewater and yoghurt or fruit and cinnamon.

Harvest is a pleasant place to eat with its whitewashed walls, lakeland photos and stripped pine tables. The atmosphere is relaxed and friendly and the serving staff are usually keen amateurs, earning enough to trek round the mountains in their spare time, and probably work off the toffee pudding!

Open: 12-2.30 Friday, 12-9.30 Saturday and Sunday, January-March. 12-2.30, 5-9 Monday-Friday, 12-9.30 Saturday and Sunday, April-December
Credit cards: none
48 seats

 ♿ 🍾 📓 🚭

Lancrigg Vegetarian Country House Hotel ✓

Easedale, Grasmere, Cumbria, LA22 9QN
☎ 09665 317
🛏 £9.50

There can't be many places where you can sit and watch rabbits playing on the lawn as you tuck into your meal. Lancrigg Country House Hotel is such a place with a wonderful setting, extensive grounds and superb views over the fells. The restaurant caters mainly for the residents, and outsiders do need to book.

The set four-course dinner is served at 7pm (try to arrive promptly, as if you are late, as we were on one occasion, you are rather hurried through your meal). There is no choice of dishes on the menu, except when it comes to the pudding, which can spoil your meal if you don't happen to fancy one of the dishes. To avoid this, just ring to check this out first.

We had a lovely nectarine starter with tarragon cream sauce, followed by a lemony lentil soup. The main course was dull — deep-fried battered vegetables with a tahini sauce. It came on cold plates, with cold noodles and so quickly went cold too. Time to cheer up when it came to the puddings though, lovely pineapple upside-down cake, blackcurrant sorbet, bananas in wine and fresh fruit salad. Coffee (decaffeinated if you wish) and mints to follow. We were unlucky with the main course, as on other visits we had an excellent aubergine bake and a colourful chick pea casserole.

A small niggle. We thought the service was a little sloppy. The wine was poured carelessly into the glasses with no chance to taste and the plates were whipped away, even when, after being late, we had 'caught up'. Lancrigg is such a delightful place, and the owners have done a great deal to make it possible for you to eat in style that I think they should give you just a little more time to relax and enjoy it. Perhaps the thing to do is stay for breakfast when you can enjoy choices of cereals, wonderful stewed fruit and mushrooms etc on toast.

Open: 7pm daily
Credit cards: none
24 seats
🍷 📝 ⊘

210

Lupton Tower

Lupton, nr Kirkby Lonsdale, Cumbria, LA6 2PR
☎ 04487 400
£10

Lupton Tower is a charming eighteenth century country house,
set in its own grounds with a lovely view over to Farleton Knot.
They try to offer you all the facilities and sophistication of a
country house too. There is comfort throughout with soft sofas
and soft lighting, log fires and good-quality tableware. The menu
is on traditional lines, but veg. and two veg. rather than meat
and two veg.! It is a set meal of four courses, but, as there is
only one sitting, you can enjoy the food at a leisurely pace.

There was a starter of avocado and cream cheese dip, followed
by carrot and orange soup with walnut bread. The main course
consisted of a baked mould with chestnuts, served with dill and
celery sauce. The accompanying vegetables were potatoes, peas
and tomatoes. The food was very well presented, tasty too. The
portions were satisfying, but not so enormous that I was left
bloated with no room for the puddings. For the dessert course,
there was a choice of quite gorgeous sweets, including a
chocolate pudding with brandy sauce, peaches and cream or a
lemon and whisky roulade. Round off your meal with coffee and
mints.

During the year, the menu does change, especially to
accommodate seasonal varieties of vegetables, but it usually
includes dishes fairly similar to those I tried. The only danger
with a set meal is that you might not like the main course, but
you could always check on what it is likely to be when you
book.

The owners (the husband serves and the wife cooks) certainly
try to please. They have taken great care with the place and
Lupton Tower shows that is *is* possible to run a sophisticated
establishment serving vegetarian food, that surely will become
popular with vegetarians and non-vegetarians alike. With all the
trimmings, the whole meal was only £9.50, which is excellent
value. It is a splendid place for special occasions and
somewhere to take the unsuspecting carnivore who expects
heavy brown stews out of heavy brown pottery!

Lupton Tower is off the A65 between the M6 and Kirkby
Lonsdale.

Open: 7.30 for 8 sitting daily
Credit cards: none
40 seats

The Mason's Arms

Strawberry Bank, Cartmel Fell, Grange-over-Sands,
LA11 6NW
☎ 04488 486
🏠 £5

You'll find The Mason's Arms on one of the myriad of small B roads that lie between the A592 (Windermere-Newby Bridge), near the southern tip of the lake, and the A5074 from Windermere. A viewpoint close by is Gummer's How. It is a pub well worth seeking out and you won't be alone as this is a popular place for both the food and beer so do go early if you want a good choice.

I arrived here in the middle of a power cut and they were *still* able to provide me with a first-class meal! I began with soup, and followed it with what would normally have been two starters — humus and mushrooms à la Grecque. These came with good bread and a large portion of mixed salad, crisp and fresh. All quite enough for a main course. It was warm enough to sit outside and enjoy the fabulous view.

Apart from the cold dishes (and when there isn't a power cut), they do a good selection of hot dishes. These vary from time to time and might include cheese, apple and onion bake, carrot and lentil loaf, aubergine and tomato casserole, vegetable biryani and Russian vegetable pie (the last two are both vegan). The portions are all very generous and there are also some hefty puds — the most ethnic being Cumberland Rum Nicky, a sort of fruity slice on a pastry base, plus honey and walnut tart, toffee and apple pudding and fudgecake.

The system with the food is to go to the bar and order and then listen for your number in anticipation. Service is fairly quick but, while you're waiting, there is time to peruse the enormous list of ales, and perhaps sample the guest beer of the week.

Many of the staff who work here are vegetarian or practically so and that counts in part for the imaginative and extensive menu. The food and the setting are first rate.

Open: 12-1.45, 6-8.45 daily
Credit cards: none
60 seats

The Moon Restaurant

129 Highgate, Kendal, Cumbria, LA9 4EN
☎ 0539 29254
🏠 £8

Warm shades of deep reds and rust give this night-time only restaurant a very cosy atmosphere and the style is like a bistro with its blackboard menu and casual service. I somehow expected *all* the food to be vegetarian, but, in fact, some meat and fish is served as well. Vegans should check the choice as, on the menu we were offered, it was quite hard to get away from cheese. It is best to eat early too as they don't take bookings, although since I visited they have opened an upstairs room where you can have pre-meal drinks as well as coffee afterwards. They will also take bookings of 12 or more upstairs for a special occasion meal.

The menu changes daily, the soups are always vegetarian, as well as two other starters such as humus or asparagus and Camembert cream. Three of the main courses are vegetarian. We had a delicious Brie, fennel and mushroom pie, with a very filling, mixed, Moon salad, comprised of five different varieties. You can choose to have a selection of hot vegetables, brown rice or the potato bake. The potato bake is sliced potato, cooked in milk and covered with cheese. The portions are generous and sustaining. I'm not really sure how anyone manages to find room for the speciality sticky toffee pudding. Other desserts were rich cheesecake (gelatine-free) and a raspberry trifle.

The Moon is a good place to meet up with friends and have a lively evening and good food, there is just the slight snag that you may have to wait a while for your meal.

Open: 6-10 Sunday-Thursday, till 11pm Friday and Saturday
40 seats

The Plough Inn

Selside, Kendal, Cumbria, LA8 9LD
☎ 053983 687
🏠 £5

The Plough is a detached stone building on the A6 north of
Kendal. Inside is a typical open-plan pub which is very
pleasant.

It has got a good reputation for food, and now offers a
reasonable choice for vegetarians, but do be prepared for a wait.
Dishes from the bar snack menu are fairly quick to arrive, but
the minimum wait for a dish on the vegetarian menu is 20
minutes and it can be longer if you go with a party of veggie
friends! They don't just get overwhelmed by vegetarians but by
large numbers as well. However, you can amuse yourself by
drinking the good traditional ale on sale.

Main-course choices are tagliatelle or bulgur wheat with
walnuts, which were excellent and came with salad and a baked
potato, or vegetable gratin, which was disappointingly bland.
The vegetable lasagne was not available the night we went. The
puddings are on traditional lines and the apple crumble was
delicious. There was cheesecake too but check as to any gelatine
content. The portions were reasonable and the whole meal was
good value.

Open: pub hours, food till 9pm
Credit cards: none
30 seats
♿ 🍷 📋 🚬

Quince and Medlar

13 Castlegate, Cockermouth, Cumbria, CA13 9EU
☎ 0900 823579
£9

Cockermouth is on the north-west edge of the Lake District and
is still popular but not quite so crowded as the central Lakeland
areas of Ambleside and Windermere. The town and the
surrounding countryside are lovely and one famous landmark is
Castlegate House, the birthplace of William Wordsworth.

I would be tempted to go to Cockermouth solely for the
pleasure of dining at the Quince and Medlar, which is a rare
treat and absolutely excellent.

The restaurant is in a listed Georgian house, up a steep hill,
close to Cockermouth Castle. There are two small rooms, both
of which are very prettily furnished and decorated in warm,
soothing colours. There are fresh flowers and pleasant tableware.
Attention to detail extends to the menu. Everything is
beautifully served with nice accompanying touches. I went with
a party so, between us, we were able to try virtually the whole
menu. For starters there was a marvellous watercress soup,
served with a home-made roll. The pâté was an unusual spiced
mixture with mung beans that came with a popadom and rice —
it was virtually a meal in itself. Another choice was a sweet and
sour aubergine caponata.

All the main courses were excellent. The Brazil Nut Crown
was a moist nut loaf mixture, served in a tiny mould, with a
little separate pot of sauce. Other choices included a slice of
hazelnut and courgette bake, again served with a pot of sauce,
or vegetables *provençale* with pasta. All the food was extremely
tasty and the portions were generous. You could order extra
baked potatoes and side salads. The salads were a treat to look
at: colourful mixtures of vegetables and fruits with little
garnishes of redcurrants and bilberries, served with a choice of
dressings. Puddings were irresistible with excellent American-
style cheesecake, delicate Normandy apple tart, and I had a
subtle pear and quince fool.

The staff let you enjoy your meal at a leisurely pace and do
not overcrowd the restaurant. It is a very special night out and
definitely worth making every effort to go. The restaurant has
only been established a short while but it is clearly a labour of
love and I hope they continue creating such wonderful food.

Don't forget to visit the loos. The ladies is one of the prettiest I've seen, and I have it on good authority that the gents is impressive too!

You do need to book, especially at weekends. Also note that they may well extend the opening times in the tourist season.

The restaurant has recently changed hands but the new owners are keeping up the high standard.

Open: 7 onwards, daily
Credit cards: none
26 seats

The Rowan Tree

Langdale Road, Grasmere, Cumbria, LA22 9SU
☎ 09665 528
🏠 £5

This small café is hidden away at the back of Grasmere, a
popular village in the heart of Lakeland. It is probably best
avoided during the height of the season as the little village and
the even smaller car park get absolutely packed. Having said
that, I managed to find a little space in August and was very
grateful for the tasty, thick lentil soup, as it was a typical cold,
wet summer's day.

You order at the counter, where there is quite a bit of food on
display to tempt you. Your meal is then brought to the table.
The soup came with good wholemeal bread. For a main course
the hot dish was quite ordinary but it was tasty and well
prepared. We had a choice of vegetable and bean bake or
cauliflower cheese or quiche. These come with a jacket potato
and salad. You can also have filled jacket potatoes as a meal on
their own.

The puddings are good — some seeming more wholesome than
others — and they have a nice home-made quality. I had the
apple and raisin crumble to follow, just to my liking being much
more fruit than crumble. There was also fruit pie, lemon
meringue and plenty of cakes on offer.

The Rowan Tree has an unflustered, homely atmosphere.
Although the decor isn't anything particularly memorable, and
the furniture looks a little shabby, the friendly welcome,
appetizing cooking aromas and good-value meal outweigh these
small niggles.

Open: 10.30-6 Monday-Friday, till 7pm Saturday and Sunday
28 seats

Sheila's Cottage

The Slack, Ambleside, Cumbria, LA22 0PL
☎ 05394 33079
🏠 £3

This is a heaven-sent place for breakfast. We feasted on fresh
orange juice and a large bowl of creamy muesli. This is made to
the traditional recipe using soaked oat flakes with chopped nuts
and seasonal fruit added. It is fresh and light, a far cry from any
commercial cereal. Just the sort of treat you always promise
yourself at home but never have time to organize. We also
tucked into toasted bara brith, and drank our way through a pot
of good coffee. This is all part of the set breakfast, which is
quite enough to sustain you until tea-time, which, by the way, is
equally good at Sheila's Cottage! All the items on the set
breakfast can be ordered separately, and there are plenty of
other calorific delights, from fairly plain scones and tea breads
to sumptuous sticky cakes and gâteaux.

Sheila's Cottage also has a few suitable lunch-time savouries.
There is a ratatouille, served with granary bread or potatoes, but
most of the other dishes rely quite heavily on dairy products.
Swiss egg special is a slice of biscotte, dipped in white wine,
covered with melted Raclette cheese and topped with a fried egg.
Other choices include a Stilton and herb pâté, served with salad
or Cheddar cheese with oatcakes, celery and apple.

It is a very pretty restaurant and great attention has been paid
to detail. The serving counter is attractively set out and
everything behind it is spotlessly clean and well organized. The
china and table ware are first class. Even the menu is so
attractive that the management ask you kindly not to take it
away as a souvenir! The staff are very welcoming. We went on
consecutive days and immediately felt as though we were
regulars!

Highly recommended.

Open: 10.30-5.30 Monday-Saturday
Credit cards: none
38 seats

🍷 📋 🚭 section

The Village Bakery

Melmerby, Penrith, Cumbria, CA10 1HE
☎ 076-881 515
🏠 £4

Halfway between Penrith and Alston is the little village of
Melmerby, set in some of the most remote English countryside.
However, remote though it is, if you are staggering along the
Penine way, escaping the crowds of the Lake District or simply
sheltering from bleak moorland, it is well worth paying a visit to
The Village Bakery there.

The restaurant is housed in a converted barn. A small
conservatory, in keeping with the style, acts as the entrance but
it is also a nice warm spot to sit when the sun peeps out.

The bakery, which has been established now for 12 years,
started by specializing in breads, cakes and pastries made from
organic, wholemeal flour. It still produces a marvellous variety
of baked goods, made from both basic and enriched doughs full
of nuts, seeds and fruit.

In addition to these, on offer are all sorts of savouries and
sweets, many of which include their own home-grown fruit and
vegetables. We had some delicious, chunky vegetable and
tomato soup, followed by salad-filled savoury sesame baps. For
the main hot dish there was a creamy vegetable pie, nut roast
and salad, or ratatouille served with a jacket potato. Lighter
meals consisted of a Baker's lunch, which featured English
country cheeses and a variety of breads, or tzatziki with pitta
bread. Their cakes included carrot cake with cream cheese or a
gluten-free chocolate and almond cake. There were sweet fruit
tarts, packed full, as well as Cumberland Rum Nicky, which is a
very sweet, local speciality.

The coffee is excellent and you can have refills if you wish,
and there is a good range of other drinks. You need to order at
the counter, then everything is brought to your table. The
service was very friendly.

The restaurant is quite simply furnished, and quite crowded
with tables. Apart from the food, there is plenty to look at as
there are leaflets on weaving courses, special walks and,
upstairs, a craft shop selling good-quality pottery, prints,
woodcuts and woollen jumpers.

I found it hard to drag myself away and took two pasties —
spinach and nut and curried vegetable — as emergency rations

for later on on the journey. Both were very good, with a light, crumbly pastry. I also bought some individual quiches, which were also delicious, and little apple pies that were generously filled with fruit.

Open: 8.30-5 Tuesday-Saturday, 9.30-5 Sunday, closed
      Monday
40 seats

Waterside Wholefoods

Kent View, Waterside, Kendal, Cumbria, LA9 4DZ
☎ 0539 29743
🏠 £3

Even though we were a bit late turning up here, the staff went out of their way to find us something to eat, and jolly good it was too! The salad was fresh, packed with all sorts of ingredients (bulgur wheat, red cabbage, pepper, carrot, cucumber, sultana, apple and celery) and the onion quiche was delicious. They make a good range of wholefood cakes, including sticky gingerbread, flapjack and almond and orange slice.

The café is in a little terrace with a wholefood shop and mountain shop. Whitewashed walls, stripped pine tables and some original works of art for sale all make it a very pleasant place to get a light meal. Those who know Waterside well have said the standard is consistently good.

Open: 9-4 Monday-Saturday
Credit cards: none
24 seats

♿ 📖 🚭

Zeffirelis

Compston Road, Ambleside, Cumbria, LA22 9AD
☎ 05394 33845
🏠 £5 Garden Room Café £10 Pizzeria

Zeffirelis is a well-designed complex with a wholefood pizzeria, café, a cinema and shopping arcade.

The Garden Room Café, in a spacious ground-floor area, has a lively decor in pastel greens and white, with loads of plants and floral prints. The café is open for coffee, frothy *cappuccino*, espresso and all the usual calorific cakes. At lunch-time there is a good savoury menu with imaginative hot dishes, such as Russian Macaroni, two or three quiches, soup, jacket potatoes and a variety of salads. You can then while away the afternoon with cream teas and pastries.

The menu changes frequently, and they are always coming up with new ideas. I listened to a fascinating discussion amongst the cooks about the trials and tribulations of wholemeal croissants.

Upstairs is the wholefood Pizzeria, which caters for an evening trade. They offer an excellent value all-in three-course meal plus a cinema ticket, but you can, of course, just go there to eat. The menu isn't limited to pizzas — there are fresh pasta dishes, chillis and often a special of the day, good starters and puddings.

Open: Garden Room Café, 10-5, closed Thursdays and from
      November to April. Pizzeria, 5-9.45, closed Tuesday
      and Wednesday and from November to April
Garden Room Café 50 seats, Pizzeria 94 seats

 Garden Room Pizzeria section

Northumbria
County Durham, Northumberland, Tyne and Wear

Northumbria has a marvellous mixture of countryside — from the remote and wild moorland, often with some wild weather to match, to the white, sandy beaches and dunes along its rugged coastline. It is a lovely area to tour, and easy too as there is little traffic. You certainly need to tour to catch any vegetarian eating places as these are few and far between.

The widest selection is to be found in Newcastle, which is a city experiencing quite a resurgence. Much of the old dockland area is being redeveloped and gentrified and it is clearly a good time for new, imaginative businesses to set up.

There are several restaurants to choose in Newcastle with a wide variety of styles. Over the rest of the area, the standard is mixed. There are some rather conventional eating places, offering a reasonable vegetarian choice, and a very individual establishment in Berwick-on-Tweed. There are a couple of totally vegetarian places too, and, certainly, I think the prize for the best one in the region must go to Priors at Barnard Castle.

Blinkers Coffee House

The Old Grammar School Stables, Hallgate, Hexham,
Northumberland, NE46 1XA
☎ 0434 606656
£4

Blinkers Coffee House is in a carefully restored stable block just
by the old Hexham Jail, now a museum and tourist information
centre, and usefully *en route* from the town car park to the
centre, which was how I discovered it.

It is clean and simple with friendly, efficient service. The
choice isn't vast but there is a definite leaning toward vegetarian
and wholefood ideas. The main hot dish was a macaroni and
ratatouille bake, that had a slightly soup-like consistency, which
didn't matter too much as it was served in a bowl, with a good
mixture of salads on the side. I tried the Welsh rarebit, asking
for it to be in brown bread. It wasn't necessary for to specify
this here, however, as it is always served on a type of local
scone-like brown bread. The cheese topping had a distinctive
mustard tang and it came with a small salad garnish. Also on
offer was a cottage cheese and peach salad. There were some
wholesome-looking cakes, but lots that weren't and doughnuts
seemed very popular when we visited.

The tables are quite packed together and unfortunately they do
allow smoking, which could get unpleasant when they are really
busy. As a quick refuelling stop, I thought Blinkers was quite
acceptable and definitely an improvement on a picnic sheltering
in a bus stop!

Open: 9.30-5.00 Monday-Saturday
Credit cards: none
44 seats

The Bluebell Inn

Crookham, Cornhill-On-Tweed, Northumberland, TD12 45H
☎ 089082 252
🏠 £4

This is a small country pub just outside Crookham in lovely, wild Northumberland. Strictly speaking, *they* shouldn't take credit for the vegetarian food, as it is all made by a local (vegetarian) and bought in!

The meals are quite simple and limited to three choices: Red Dragon Pie, lentil cannelloni and cottage parcels, which were puff pastry cases filled with vegetables. The food was tasty, though a little dry due to the reheating. There was an adequate side-salad. What *was* useful was that all ingredients were listed so you feel reassured about your meal. The owners felt that, because of the demand for vegetarian meals, they would keep a choice on the menu even if they were unable to buy in.

Open: 12-2, 7-8 daily, except closed Wednesday evenings
Credit cards: none

Café Procope

35 The Quayside, Newcastle upon Tyne, NE1 3JE
☎ 091-232 3848
🏠 £6

This café cum restaurant is near the Quayside. Inside, the subtle lighting and soft music, ranging from Ella Fitzgerald to Mozart, and Tom Waits to Bessie Smith, create a restful ambiance for eating. Lunchtimes attract both local workers and tourists and in the evening there's a good mixture of people. All the food served is made on the premises.

Starters and snacks include falafels, humus, tamari mushrooms, and hot croissants with various fillings. Don't miss the latkes — lovely, traditional Jewish potato pancakes served with spicy apple relish.

There are usually four main courses to choose from and these change roughly every four months. We had vegetable fritters with an excellent gado gado sauce and wholemeal tagliatelle with pesto, cheese and pine nuts. Other choices were a herb ku-ku (a Middle Eastern spiced omelette) and a gumbo with okra and other vegetables in a creamy, garlic sauce. They always try to have something in the main-course line that is suitable for vegans.

Their home-made puds are great and these change more frequently. Our chocolate mousse was rich and alcoholic, and the cheesecake heavenly.

The wine list here is well chosen and there are some very good steam beers, plus soft drinks and herbal teas.

Everything at Café Procope adds up to a lively night out, and certainly one that could be enjoyed by meat eaters too.

Open: 9.30-10.30 Tuesday-Saturday, 10-5 Sunday
Credit cards: none
45 seats
 ♿ 🚼 📷 🚭 section

Edoardo's

6-7 Drury Lane, Cloth Market, Newcastle upon Tyne,
NE1 1HL
☎ 091-261 7608
🏠 £6

Edoardo Giacomini greets you personally at this comfortable
city-centre restaurant with its 80 per cent vegetarian menu, and
the rest of his staff are equally friendly and ready to help you
with your meal.

We had a delicious spinach and rice soup as a starter instead
of the more predictable corn on the cob. The main courses with
this Italian menu are various pizzas and pasta. The folded
Calzone pizza was well prepared and the broccoli and cheese
filling very succulent. The cannelloni was also tasty. All the
food is cooked to order by Edoardo in his open-plan kitchen
and he stresses that good food only comes from using good
ingredients. Certainly what we had bore this out.

Do leave room for the wonderful 'Torte De La Casa' — a
liqueur-soaked sponge, made to his mother's recipe. The coffee
was good, so too the nip of brandy, especially as the bottle was
left on the table!

Open: 12-2.30, 5.30-12.00 Monday-Wednesday, till 1.00
        Thursday-Saturday
50 seats

Funnywayt'makaliving

53 West Street, Berwick-upon-Tweed, TD15 1AS
☎ 0289 308827
£11.75 set price

It is not just the name that is interesting about this restaurant. It is a one-woman operation, run by Elizabeth Middlemiss. She does all the cooking, serving and clearing herself.

It is essential to book in the evening as there is a set menu and you do need to ask for a vegetarian meal. However, it is no trouble to her as she cooks for vegetarians at lunch-time.

We had fresh asparagus and a delicious chestnut cream soup. The main course was stuffed pancakes with a tasty vegetable filling, followed by a light, fresh fruit sorbet. Everything was well prepared and most beautifully presented. The restaurant does not have a licence to sell alcoholic drinks but, if you pay Elizabeth £1.00 corkage she welcomes you bringing your own wine. Funnywayt'makaliving has a homely feel to it, but it is elegant at the same time as there are lovely table settings and some nice antique pieces. It is a thoroughly enjoyable experience to come for a meal here.

Open: 12-3 Monday-Wednesday, till 8 Friday and Saturday
Credit cards: none
24 seats

Heartbreak Soup

77 The Quayside, Newcastle upon Tyne, NE1 3DG
☎ 091-222 1701
🏠 £7

Cult features prominently on the menu here. The name of the restaurant is taken from an American cult comic *Love and Rockets*, all about a small, fictitious town in Mexico. Inside the restaurant, the decor features trendy Mexican designs, and magazines such as *The Face* are around for browsing.

The Quayside is an up-and-coming area of Newcastle — relatively quiet in the day, but lively at night with lots of pubs, night-clubs and, of course, restaurants. This place appeals to the young, outgoing crowd.

Mexican food is served here, of course. Snacks, such as tortilla chips and guacamole, corn on the cob for starters, with traditional tostadas and enchilladas with spicy bean fillings as main courses. The best dish is the rich bean stew with a beer and cheese sauce. My only niggles are that the food could be better presented. Most of the desserts are bought in and 'Death by Chocolate' might be more appropriately named 'Death by E Numbers', whilst the Pina Colada is sinfully alcoholic. However, the staff are friendly and laid back, in keeping with the style.

Open: 12-3, 6-12 daily
70 seats
 section

Priors ✓

7 The Bank, Barnard Castle, County Durham, DL12 8PH
☎ 0833 38141
🏠 £4

Priors' restaurant is behind a most attractive and interesting fine art and craft shop. You can browse (and buy) original pictures, etchings and so on should there be a queue at the small counter. The place is popular — deservedly so as the food is varied, imaginative, with a large selection so everyone is sure to find something they like.

The menu is displayed on a large board and it is quite a challenge to match the descriptions to the dishes displayed before you. Best to go by what catches your eye! The food you choose is then microwaved and brought to your table. We tried a lovely pasta and walnut dish — light and tasty, bound together with a good mushroom flavour, served with a tomato sauce that was, unfortunately, somewhat dried up as it had been over-microwaved. There were also some very tasty looking quiches. Not just the standard dairy type either, but mixtures such as spicy lentil. In addition, there were pizzas and a good range of salads. Puddings and cakes were irresistible. I was even offered a choice of Bakewell tart (my favourite) either traditional or apricot, and there was a thick apple pie — thick on apples that is, not pastry — plus a dazzling array of cakes and biscuits. There were plenty of drinks on offer, too — soft and alcoholic.

Looking over at some of the other tables, I envied the chap who had chosen a ploughman's lunch. It came with a really good chunk of cheese, decent bread, salad and an apple!

Priors did try opening in the evenings, too, which proved very hard work for little reward, and so they have decided, sadly, not to continue with this. However, they are still doing the monthly gourmet dinners. These are held on the last Friday of each month and you get a set meal for £8.50. They use this evening to try out some interesting international dishes, and you can choose from at least three main courses.

The atmosphere is quite different from that of the day: the lighting is lowered, there is table service and, as you have the table for the whole evening, you can just relax and enjoy your meal at leisure.

These evenings have been very popular so you do need to book ahead. Maybe in time they will be encouraged to try the regular evening openings again. There didn't seem to be any opposition.

Open: 10-5 Monday-Friday, till 6 Saturday, 6.30 Sunday,
        closed Sundays from November to Easter
50 seats

      section

Red Herring Café

4 Studley Terrace, Fenham, Newcastle upon Tyne, NE4 5AM
☎ 091-272 3484
🏠 £4

Recently opened as a workers co-operative, Andy, Claire, James, Maria, Nigel, Paul and Victor welcome you to this community café about five minutes out of the city centre. It is pleasantly decorated with a relaxed atmosphere.

A feature of the Red Herring Café is its bakery, which uses a traditional coke-fired oven. They produce a marvellous range of breads using 100 percent organic flours, plus wholemeal croissants and *pain au chocolat*. Apart from these lighter snacks, there is a good range of wholesome meals and everything is home cooked. Starters include a tasty broccoli soup, or a wine and nut pâté. There are unusual main courses influenced by a variety of international cuisines: spicey tempeh, pilau rice, borek filled with feta cheese, all served with fresh crisp salads. There are snacks such as quiche, pasties, pizza, garlic bread and jacket potatoes on offer as well as trifle, crumble and delicious Hunza apricots with cashew cream. Vegans are well catered for here.

Although the Red Herring Café is not licenced to sell alcoholic drinks, you can bring your own with you if you like.

This co-operative is certainly trying to approach the business of running a café with imagination. Apart from enjoying the food, you may be lucky to go on an evening when there is live music or a poetry reading. On Sundays the Chileans in the group provide authentic Latin American food.

Overlooking a park, with its light and airy atmosphere, the Red Herring is definitely worth a visit.

Open: 10-8 Tuesday-Sunday
Credit cards: none
40 seats
♿ 🍽 ✏ 🚭 section

Scotland

The choice for vegetarians north of the border is already varied but it also seems to be increasing further. Edinburgh, hardly surprisingly, has the widest range of places with some excellent wholefood cafés as well as authentic Indian food and interesting snacks served in galleries and coffee shops. The eating scene in Glasgow has improved for vegetarians. Perhaps the most well-established place is the Ubiquitous Chip.

Apart from these two cities, places throughout the rest of Scotland crop up rather unexpectedly in Inverness, Ullapool and Kyle of Lochalsh. Further north, you are well advised to take your own sandwiches. Despite the lack of restaurants here do not miss out on exploring the Highlands as the countryside is not only unspoiled but practically deserted.

Babbity Bowster

16-18 Blackfriars Street, Glasgow, Scotland, G1 1PE
☎ 041-552 5055
🏠 £5

Hustle, bustle and a friendly welcome greet you at Babbity
Bowster. This overcomes any impression you may have of it
being too crowded and smoky to stay!

The menu is fairly meaty, right from the full Scottish breakfast
through to the venison hot-pot, but, at every meal, there are
vegetarian options. There is muesli to start the day, light meals
of baked courgette, filled jacket potatoes and garlic-buttered
mushrooms, and one main-course choice of vegetarian loaf.

There are some tempting puddings, too, such as honey cake
and apple strudel, and an interesting cheese board.

Adding to the atmosphere is a programme of events featured
from time to time in the Gallery restaurant, as well as live music
on winter Sundays and occasional poetry evenings. There is
some limited accommodation too.

Babbity Bowster isn't especially good for vegetarians, but it is
useful to know about because it is the sort of place you could
go with a mixed party for a lively time and not get stuck with
the customary omelette.

Open: 8-10.30, 12-3 Monday-Friday, 8-10.30, 12-3, 5-late
      Monday-Saturday
100 seats
♿ 🍾 📋 🚬

The Baked Potato Shop

56 Cockburn Street, Edinburgh, Lothian, EH1 1PB
☎ 031-225 7572
🏠 £2

As you would guess from the name, the main items on sale here
are baked potatoes with an enormous variety of fillings. The café
has a seventies vegetarian air, with stripped pine, loads of
posters, music and an unpretentious, friendly atmosphere.

   The emphasis — with only six seats — is on take-away food,
and the queues get quite long at peak eating times.

   You can choose to have hot or cold fillings, ranging from the
standard cheese, coleslaw or beans to the more unusual, such as
the delicious mushroom risotto.

   The Baked Potato Shop is a good place for grabbing a bite if
you are dashing round the Festival, or, indeed, any other time
you happen to be in Edinburgh.

Open: 10-11 daily
Credit cards: none
6 seats

♿ 🗘 🍽

Basil's √

184 Dumbarton Road, Glasgow, Scotland, G11 6UN
☎ 041-337 1416
 £6

Although plain and simple, Basil's has a stylish feel with good
decor and lighting. The menu, too, is attractively presented and
the food is well prepared.

We had to wait quite some time for our lunch as it was not
only fairly busy, but the service is a little amateur and not
totally attentive. However, we were very refreshed by a non-
alcoholic spritzer (a long drink of organic apple juice, diluted
with sparkling water!)

There was an unusual smoked tofu and leek starter, as well as
an excellent olive pâté, served in a little ramekin with oat cakes
and a salad garnish. The main courses were a tasty lasagne,
which was piping hot, and a nut roast painstakingly decorated
with stripes of sesame and poppy seeds, served with a miso
gravy. Both these came with a so-called special salad, which was
disappointingly ordinary. A better bet might have been the
baked potato deluxe, which was the choice of several people
near us. It looked colourful and brimful of unusual ingredients.

For pudding I had the cheesecake which was heavenly.

Basil's is smart enough to be a venue for a special lunch or
evening meal, but also friendly and relaxed enough to pop into
for a light meal.

Open: 11-11 Monday, 11, 6.30-11 Tuesday, 11-11 Wednesday-
      Saturday (last orders 9.30)
Credit cards: none
40 seats
♿♿ 🍶 ▱ 🚭 section

Boxers

18 Howe Street, Edinburgh, Lothian EH3 6TD
☎ 031-225 7225
day £4, evening £7

Boxers is housed in a typical, grey, stone, Edinburgh building.
It must once have been a rather grand town dwelling, though
the high ceilings are practically all that remain of its past
grandeur. These give a spacious, airy feel to the restaurant.

During the day, there is a buffet-style lunch. The vegetarian
selection is quite basic with choices limited to soup, pâté,
macaroni cheese and baked potatoes.

It is best to eat early, as the main courses are kept hot by
means of a warm light system and tend to dry out. The salads
here are fresh and there is a good choice of standard mixtures:
beans, Oriental, green, rice, tomato, and carrot.

For afters, there is fresh fruit salad and a good selection of
home-baked cakes and scones.

Newspapers are provided so you feel encouraged to dawdle
over your meal. It is a pleasant place to have a simple lunch.

In the evening Boxers reopens as a Spanish restaurant. Some
vegetarian tapas are provided, such as tortillas and mixed
peppers.

Open: 10-5, 6-10.30 Monday-Saturday
50 seats

 day, evening

239

Brookes Wine Bar

75 Castle Street, Inverness, Invernesshire, IV2 3EA
☎ 0463 225662
♉ £6

It was good to find something a little different and more
wholesome in Inverness than the ubiquitous pizza. Brookes is a
popular place so the vegetarian food does run out, as we found
when we went back for seconds of their delicious wholemeal
bread only to find that it had all gone!

There are usually a couple of hot dishes to choose from, such
as mushroom and nut loaf, or stuffed pancakes. There are also
the more standard vegetable flans and jacket potatoes. The
range of salads is good. There are usually four on display at a
time which are replaced as the bowls empty. Try to wait to
choose when there is a full selection. There are coleslaws, and
pasta-based salads as well as some imaginative mixtures of
sweet and savoury, such as melon with avocado and grapefruit.
The soup, for example courgette and fennel, is sometimes
vegetarian but it is best to check.

The puddings on offer may include gelatine, but the
management were aware that this is not part of a vegetarian
diet, and are always willing to make fruit salad.

You help yourself to cutlery and cold food, but hot food will
be brought to your table.

Brookes is a friendly, lively place.

Open: 11-11 Monday-Wednesday, Saturday, Sunday, 1-11
        Thursday and Friday (last orders 10)
Credit cards: none
70 seats
🍾 ⧄ ⊘ section

The Ceilidh Place

West Argyll Street, Ullapool, Invernesshire, IV26 2TY
☎ 0854 2103
🛏 £5 coffee shop, £13 restaurant

Ullapool nestles under the hills on the side of the Loch Broom
and, from the bay, you look out to sea toward the Summer
Isles.

It is the last place you are likely to see a crowd, and, you
would have thought, unlikely to offer a vegetarian meal if you
are penetrating to the far North West of the Scottish mainland.
Yet it is really worth making the trip here thanks to the Ceilidh
Place, which comprises a hotel, a formal restaurant, with set
meal, a coffee shop, for more casual eating, and club house, for
drinking plus live music. The food is mainly wholefood with
about half the menu being vegetarian.

In the coffee shop, they are open for drinks and cakes at the
start of the day, then they have two or three main dishes ready
at about 12 o'clock, for example vegetable curry or quiche.
These 'Hot specials' change at 5 o'clock, so you can come back
for a different meal in the evening. There are usually also seven
to eight salads to choose from, jacket potatoes, some safe soups
and various cakes — including a very good vegan fruit cake —
and puddings, plus good coffee.

To get your food, you queue at the large counter. I found the
service a bit chaotic sometimes, with, seemingly, lots of activity
for not much of a result. Maybe it was my leftover urban
impatience!

On the set menu offered in the restaurant, you'll probably find
a couple of choices for starters and main course. The food is
brought to your table.

To tempt you further, in the centre of the room a large table is
laid with all the desserts and a selection of cheeses. Then you
end the meal with coffee and sweets.

Overall the Ceilidh Place is attractive, relaxed and friendly.

Open: 9.30-9 daily in coffee shop, 7-9 (last orders) daily in
       restaurant
50 seats in coffee shop, 40 seats in restaurant

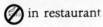  coffee shop ⌷ restaurant

🚭 in restaurant

The Gallery Café

The Scottish National Gallery of Modern Art, Belford Road,
Edinburgh, Lothian, EH4 3DR
☎ 031-332 8600
🏠 £4

The Gallery Café gets my recommendation as a place to go for a
peaceful oasis in the middle of Edinburgh, especially during the
hurly burly of the August festivities.

The interior of the café is spacious, but it is best to go into
the garden patio. Even in faintly good weather, it is most
enjoyable going outside. The place is well looked after and there
are sculptures to gaze at too.

As to the food, the menu for vegetarians consists of soup and
a choice of two main courses. The vegetable plait was great,
made from a very light filo-like pastry and filled with a creamy,
vegetable sauce. The whole thing was tasty and delicate. Other
choices include snacks, such as cheesy, egg-filled croissants, and
a range of about six standard salads.

There are also all the usual cakes — banana cake, carrot cake
— shortbreads and scones, as well as a wonderful pavlova.

You select your meal at the counter, which can get a bit slow
if a queue builds up.

Open: 10.30-4.30 Monday-Saturday, 2.00-4.30 Sunday
Credit cards: none
50 seats
♿ 🍼 🍽 🚭 section

Helios Fountain

7 Grassmarket, Edinburgh, Lothian EH1 2HY
☎ 031-229 7884
🏠 £3

At Helios Fountain you have the café, which serves decent food, and the added benefit of a decent bookshop. The shop is at the front and the café at the rear.

The café menu has been developed in accordance with Rudolf Steiner philosophies, so they use organically or biodynamically-grown foods. The ingredients are all wholefood. Having said that, the food is simple and the menu is quite small. There is a choice of soups, main courses, such as savoury loaf or casserole, a good selection of salads and some lovely puddings and cakes. Everything looked nice and fresh and was tasty to eat.

The Helios Fountain is a place well worth visiting.

Open: 10-6 Monday-Saturday, 11-5 Sunday, 10-8 August and December
35 seats

Henderson's Salad Table ✓

94 Hanover Street, Edinburgh, Lothian, EH2 1DR
☎ 031-225 2131
 £5

Henderson's scarcely needs any publicity as the restaurant has
been steadily selling good, vegetarian wholefood for the last 25
years and have become something of an institution, rather like
The Mousetrap!

Second-generation vegetarians will no doubt feel, as I do, that
the place has got rather stuck decor-wise in the sixties, with its
artex walls and wooden wall-hangings, which don't do much to
relieve the claustrophobic feeling of the basement. I could
scarcely believe that they had just redecorated, as it's all just the
same!

Henderson's serve the food — all made on the premises —
canteen-style with plenty of hot and cold dishes on display. I
prefer to go in the morning when the food and the place is
really fresh — inevitably things get a little tired at the end of a
long, busy day.

For breakfast you can indulge in hot croissants, delicious
muesli or soaked fruit mixtures for £1.40, plus juices and coffee.

The savoury menu, which is served through to the evening,
includes simple hot dishes, such as ratatouille, more elaborate
stuffed vegetables, snack items, such as burgers, rissoles, and
pasties, plus a choice of 20 salads. These are sold at 70p per
portion so it becomes quite expensive if you want to end up
with a decent mixture of more than three.

There is a good choice of puddings, cakes and squares and, if
you have room, vegetarian Scottish cheeses and biscuits!

In the wine bar at lunch-time there is also a food counter.
Even though I have been to Henderson's many times, I was
never aware of this bar upstairs as the entrance is in Thistle
Street. It is generally quieter here, with classical music playing
in the background but the choices of food are the same. The
wine bar may be more suitable than the restaurant for anyone
who finds the crowds in the basement areas somewhat
oppressive.

Open: 8-10.45 Monday-Saturday, 9-9 Sunday during Festival
250 seats
 section

Highland Designworks
Wholefood Café

Plockton Road, Kyle of Lochalsh, IV40 8DA
☎ 0599 4428 (0599 4388)
🏠 £4 day, £7 evening

The train journey from Inverness to the Kyle of Lochalsh is
absolutely delightful and my experience of it was made even
more worthwhile because we were greeted at the station by a
notice advertising this local wholefood restaurant.

The rather grandly named Highland Design Centre, which
houses a pleasant, spacious restaurant with beautiful views
towards Skye and Raasay, is about half a mile out of Kyle on
the Plockton Road.

The style here is similar to that of many wholefood
restaurants, with counter service during the day and a largely
predictable menu. However, what was on offer was well
presented and flavoursome. There was a choice of soups, a hot
dish, such as shepherd's beany bake, or vegetarian lasagne, a
choice of six salads and a variety of lighter meals. Aduki burgers
are served in a roll with salad, and I had a good, tasty slice of
pizza.

The restaurant can get hectic in the height of summer, but the
staff are friendly and efficient.

In the evenings, they try to create a more relaxed atmosphere
by changing the lighting, music and style of service.

The evening menu offers a choice of four or five simple
starters, such as humus or garlic mushrooms, several main
courses, one of the most popular being a pine nut loaf with
herb and lemon stuffing.

For dessert there are gelatine-free mousses, and homely fruit
pies with interesting combinations, such as banana and rhubarb.
The menu is 85 per cent vegetarian as they serve a couple of
fish dishes, but, thanks to the fact that most of the staff are
vegetarian, they ensure that the cooking never gets mixed up.

Open: 10.30-7 Tuesday-Saturday March and April, 10-9.30
      daily end May to October, closed January and February
34 seats plus outdoor seating

🏔 ♿ 🍴 day 🗒 evening 🚭

Kalpna

2-3 St Patrick Square, Edinburgh, Lothian, EH8 9ES
☎ 031-667 9890
£7

Kalpna is an exemplary Indian vegetarian restaurant, serving Gujerati and South Indian cuisine.

Classic starters consist of bhel poori, samosas (highly recommended) and more unusual dishes, such as kachori, which are spiced lentil savouries, and tikkia, a cake made from potatoes and coconut, served with a tamarind sauce. There is a wonderful bhajee made with aubergines, spinach and tomato, spiced with fenugreek and asafoetida.

For main courses, the dosa, light rice pancakes, are good and the mughal kufta curry with cheese curd, nuts and onions in a hot spicy sauce is delicious (kufta are small vegetable cutlets.)

All the dishes have interesting blends of flavours. If you are new to this style of food, it is worth trying one of the thalis, a traditional set meal where you get a little taste of many different dishes.

Cleanse your palate after your meal with one of the refreshing home-made fresh fruit sorbets, or have a treat of rich halava or kulfi, an Indian ice-cream. Herb teas are also available.

The decor at Kalpna is simple and, funnily enough almost Italian in style. The service is quite relaxed.

The reputation of this restaurant has grown tremendously, and it is very popular in the evenings — to the point of almost running out of food during the Festival. At lunch-time it is more peaceful and you can be sure that all the dishes on the menu will be available.

Open: 12-2 5.30-11 Monday-Saturday
70 seats

◣ VISA ❧ ♿ 🍶 ◻ ⊘

Sunflower Country Kitchen

4 South Charlotte Street, Edinburgh, Lothian, EH2 4AW
☎ 031-220 1700
🏠 £5

When the restaurant first opened some six years ago, an unusual feature was that every dish was calorie counted. It could be seen as a dieter's delight — or nightmare! The fashion for this has died down somewhat and now people just come in to enjoy the wholesome food.

The menu remains the same right through the day, offering a selection of fairly basic hot dishes, such as bean and tomato casserole, wholewheat macaroni cheese or nut roast. There are about 16 salads to choose from, with several imaginative mixtures, and, for anyone still counting their calories, there are some sugar-free fruit flans and muffins.

The decor is simple with pine seating and white walls and good use of plants as table dividers, which gives the place a fresh, summery feel.

Open: 8-7 Monday-Saturday* (and on Sundays during the
      Edinburgh Festival)
Credit cards: none
240 seats

*Note that during the festival they tend to open later, so check times before you go.

The Third Eye Centre

350 Sauchiehall Street, Glasgow, Scotland, G2 3JD
☎ 041-332 7521
£4

Don't miss The Third Eye. Having said that, it is easy to do —
we walked past it three times before finally realizing that the
door to the café is behind a bookshop and it is also the way in
to the gallery and theatre!

The café itself is large, plain and quite utilitarian with seating
at solid wooden tables. They welcome you for meals throughout
the day, and we arrived halfway between brunch and lunch.
There is a small, fairly predictable menu with four main courses,
of hot-pots and stuffed vegetables, soup, and a good selection of
salads and sweet biscuits and cakes, including a rather delicious
apple puff.

The service was pleasant and the general atmosphere friendly.
Though it is not a place for a special occasion, it is good for a
meal out on shopping trips or somewhere to go for a light meal
before going to one of the shows here.

Open: 10-9 Tuesday-Saturday, 2-5.30 Sunday
Credit cards: none
80 seats

The Ubiquitous Chip

12 Ashton Lane (off Byres Road) Glasgow, Scotland, G12 8SB
☎ 041-334 5007
🏠 £10

This is a trendy restaurant and wine bar complex, down a tiny cobbled lane in the University area of Glasgow.

The main restaurant here is a mass of plants, giving an extravagantly green feel to the whole place. Sadly the menu isn't green to match, and there are really only one or two choices for vegetarians amongst the meat and fish. What is there, though, is imaginative, well-presented and expensive. It struck me as the sort of place to go with meat-eaters, as long as they were paying!

There is also a bar upstairs where, at lunch-time, there is a good choice of salads and some lighter, cheaper, vegetarian options.

Open: 12-2.30, 5.30-11 daily
120 seats

The Vine Leaf

131 South Street, St Andrews, Fife, Scotland, KY16 9UN
☎ 0334 77497
🏠▪ £11

Considering the size of this little restaurant, and the fact that it is virtually a two-man operation, they offer an amazing range of foods — not only accommodating vegetarians, but serving traditional, meat-based meals as well.

The menu changes daily, depending very much on what is available locally.

There are generally three or four suitable starters, often including a vegetarian soup. For main courses there might be hazel and cashew roast with sweet pepper sauce, tortellini with fresh herb sauce, spinach roulade or Asian curry with raita.

Wicked puddings include strawberry meringue devil or white chocolate Drambuie mousse, but a speciality is the home-made ice-cream. A popular one is gooseberry and sweet geranium, made from fresh fruit bought in season.

The Vine Leaf is a comfortable, intimate restaurant with friendly owners who will certainly make sure you enjoy your evening out.

Open: 7-9.15 Tuesday-Saturday
Credit cards: none
30 seats

 ♿ 🍷 📓 🚭

Wales

This is a vast region, but both North and South Wales are very well provided for when it comes to good places to find vegetarian food. I felt on my trips that I was always within reach of somewhere good to eat. This did sometimes mean a bit of a drive, but as the main traffic jams are caused by sheep, travel is quick and easy. It was encouraging to find both well-established vegetarian places that were clearly thriving as well as brand new ventures that were either completely vegetarian or where the proprietors felt it was essential to offer interesting non-meat choices.

Many of the vegetarian places reviewed are only open in the day. They offer cheap, basic food and simple surroundings. The commitment in these places to good food was evident. Much use was made of organic products and high-quality wholefoods, particularly in Small Planet, The Great Oak Café, Sage and The Quarry Shop. There are, however, also a variety of places for more sophisticated evening eating. I've reviewed several wine bars, all of which had lively atmospheres and worthwhile selections of food. To complete the list there are some traditional hotels and charming tea rooms as well as one of the few places in this book where you need to warn them you are vegetarian, however it is included as it is also an excellent place to stay.

Apart from eating places, there are some excellent wholefood shops attached to several of the restaurants mentioned, as well as ones in Bangor and Llandrindod Wells.

The Armless Dragon Restaurant

97 Wyverne Road, Cathays, Cardiff, Wales
☎ 0222 382357
🏠 £11

This excellent informal restaurant, near Cardiff University, serves
a wide range of wholesome vegetarian meals. Vegans are well
catered for, too.

The surroundings are interesting with unusual decor and
displays of original works of art, and the service from the
uniformed staff is friendly and efficient.

Many of the dishes are quite original and imaginative and
could probably tempt some carnivores away from the meat and
fish menu. There are starters, such as artichoke aïoli, and Thai-
style mushroom and almond toast, with stir-fry samphire and
tofu as a main course. Good use is made of local and seasonal
products.

Despite being well-established this is a trendy place for an
evening out.

Open: 12.30-2.15, 7.30-10.30 Monday-Friday,
          12-30-2.15, 7.30-11 Saturday
50 seats

The Bubbling Kettle

Opposite Miners Bridge, Betws-y-Coed, Gwynedd, Wales,
LL24 0BY
☎ 06902 667
🏠 £3

The food on offer at The Bubbling Kettle is all home-made fare,
plain and wholesome. The vegetarian food consists of lasagne,
nut roasts, quiches and vegetable curry (non-vegetarian options
are plaice and chips and so on), but it is freshly cooked and
reasonably priced. There are snack items, too, such as jacket
potatoes, and scones, apple pie and home-made cakes. If you
would like a glass of wine with your meal you will need to bring
your own as the café is unlicensed, but the owners are quite
happy for you to do this.

The owners are not vegetarian, but certainly anxious to please
and understand vegetarian requirements. They are also now
hoping to offer some vegan food.

Open: 11.30-5.30 Monday-Thursday, Saturday and Sunday
Credit cards: none
20 seats
♿ 📓 🚭 section

Chandler's Brasserie

Trefriw, Gwynedd, Wales, LL27 0JH
☎ 0492 640991
🛏 £10

Trefriw is between Betws-y-Coed and Conwy, near Colwyn Bay.
Chandler's has been set up recently by a trio trying to use the
best foods and freshest ingredients without gimmicks. It takes its
name from the old chandler's shop that used to be on the site
and some of the original features, such as the open fireplace and
beautiful floor of local slate remain, adding greatly to the
atmosphere. There is little decoration on the walls, just a few
very interesting, coloured,seventeenth century gingerbread
moulds. The furniture is simple too — old school desks
converted into dining tables. The plain but pleasant
surroundings leave you to concentrate on the food which is
good.

There is always a good selection of starters, some delicious
home-made rolls and a main course choice for vegetarians,
which might be vegetable moussaka, kebabs, courgette *gougère*
or salad platter and dips. Everything is well presented.

Chandler's is not the place to go for a hurried snack as the
dishes are prepared specially for you, but the friendly welcome
and attentive service make you feel well looked after and create
a relaxed mood so you really enjoy the evening. There are not
too many places that I know of that reach this level of
sophistication in North Wales and they deserve to succeed.

When I visited they were discussing slightly different opening
times to cater for the different demands during the day and
evening, so it is advisable to ring.

Open: 12-2 Monday, 12-2, 7-10 (last orders) Tuesday-Sunday*
36 seats

*Open evenings only Tuesday-Saturday, Sunday lunch from September to
May.

The Cobblers

3 Church Street, Llandybie, Ammanford, Wales
☎ 0269-850 540
🏠 £10

This restaurant is housed in a large old terrace house and takes its name from the cobbler's shop that used to be on the site. The interior decor is lovely with a mixture of stripped pine and antiques, and pretty lace table-cloths.

The atmosphere is quite relaxed, the service efficient, but not hurried, and we were invited to 'stay on' after our meal to enjoy the coffee and savour the evening's gastronomic experience. The food was delicious.

A five-course vegetarian meal is provided with an emphasis on wholefoods, and many organic products are used. We started with an interesting laver bread roulade, followed by pancakes, stuffed with a strongly flavoured cheese sauce. The main course consisted of a very good bean and nut casserole with a choux pastry topping, and stuffed peppers, though we felt the filling was a little undercooked. Smoked tofu kebabs are sometimes available as another choice. These are served with salad or hot vegetables. I liked the fact that there was a choice of main courses as sometimes with a set menu, if you don't like the central part of the meal, and have no options, you can feel disappointed.

There was a choice with the puddings, too. Plums stewed in red wine, wholemeal tart with an unusual orange flower pastry, and carrot cake. I even found room for the tempting little muesli biscuits served with the cheese course.

Overall, the meal was wonderful value and made a most enjoyable evening.

Open: 12-2, 7-11 Tuesday-Saturday
20-45 seats

VISA 🍷 📋 🚭

Cwmtwrch Farm Hotel and Four Seasons Country Restaurant

Nantgaredig, Carmarthen, Dyfed, Wales, SA3 7NY
☎ 026788 238
🛏 £11

My heart sank at first when I got the usual 'I can rustle up a vegetarian meal for you', but our meal at Cwmtwrch was one of the best rustled-up ones I've had!

The restaurant is in a converted cow shed, but the result is very effective and comfortable. The old wide entrance has been kept, but has been extended with a large conservatory. The decor is quite simple — old pine tables, whitewashed walls — but there are plenty of interesting pictures and mementoes around, including a most unusual corner dresser. In the centre of the room is a large pine table that gradually gets covered with a tempting array of puddings as the evening wears on. The kitchen, visible from the restaurant, is filled with the biggest Aga I have ever seen.

There is a set menu of four courses, including cheese.

We started with halves of melon, stuffed with grapes. For the main course there was a piping hot pasta dish — tagliatelle in a light, herby, tomato sauce, served in a large pottery dish, that fitted snugly into a basket to keep it warm. The accompanying salad was a mixture of unusual leaves with a flavoursome dressing.

For pudding I had a delicious, fresh, nectarine salad, but there was a large meringue confection and chocolate cake that would have sorely tempted anyone with a sweet tooth.

At Cwmtwrch, apart from the restaurant, there are six rooms for bed and breakfast. The high standards of the restaurant are evident in the facilities offered. The rooms are delightful, clean and comfortable, and the breakfast is superb: good muesli, fruit *compote*, decent wholemeal bread, a choice of spreads and excellent coffee.

Overall there is a homely, relaxed atmosphere, with great attention to detail.

Although Cwmtwrch is one of the few place in this book where you will have to give notice that you are vegetarian, I felt it deserves a mention, firstly because the food is so good and, secondly because it is an excellent place to stay.

Open: 7.30pm-9.30 daily
Credit cards: none
44 seats

Dylanwad Da

2 Smithfield Street, Dolgellau, Gwynedd, Wales, LL40 1BS
☎ 0341-422 870
🏠 £10

The choice for vegetarians at Dylanwad Da is small but worth
mentioning as the food is excellent.

We started with a marvellous vegetable soup, well-flavoured
and garnished with cream and parsley.

The main course was a risotto that was presented in half a
pineapple shell and crammed full of a mixture of exotic nuts,
pecans, brazils and almonds. It was very good.

The menu changes monthly, but there is quite a reliance on
dairy products. Past starters have included onion soup, with
traditional French cheese topping, and *oeuf cocotte*. Main courses
have included such delights as *crêpes vegetariennes*, which hardly
needs translation. These are filled with different vegetables and
served with a tomato, orange and rosemary sauce. Vegans would
be well advised to phone and discuss what is suitable.

The decor here is smart, and there are nice touches of fresh
flowers on the tables. The waitresses were delightful.

Open: 7-9.30 Monday-Saturday
Credit cards: none
34 seats

🍷📓🚭

Food for Good

Rhyl Library, Church Street, Rhyl, Clwyd, Wales, LL18 3AA
☎ 0745 344971
🏠 £4

The wonderfully varied menu in this modern café definitely makes it worth a visit to Rhyl.

Food for Good is run by a women's co-operative and has been going for about 18 months. It is part of the library and exhibition centre in an attractive, purpose-built building. The café is open-plan with a triangular serving counter and the kitchen is visible behind — a very good way of ensuring a place stays spotless! The system is that you order at the counter, and the food is brought over to your table.

The menu changes daily, though try the cheese profiteroles with ratatouille if they are on offer. What remains constant is the quality of the food — home-made and very fresh, but, just occasionally, not piping hot. There are different soups, pâtés, casseroles, pies and interesting salads, which you serve yourself, and a good choice of cakes. The food is very nearly 100 per cent vegetarian, but the occasional tuna sandwich appears. Unfortunately they are not licensed to sell wine, but you can bring your own to consume on the premises if you want to. The prices are reasonable and they are doing everything they can to make wholesome foods as appealing as all the brightly-coloured fare normally sold at the seaside. Recently they won a healthy eating award from the Welsh Heartbeat Campaign. A small selection of wholefoods are also on sale.

Open: 10-7 Monday-Friday, 10-4.30 Saturday
Credit cards: none
50 seats
♿ ⏏ ⊘ section

Gales Wine and Food Bar

18 Bridge Street, Llangollen, Clwyd, Wales, LL70 8PF
☎ 0978 860089
🏠 £6

Gales Wine and Food Bar has been established for over ten
years. During this time they have expanded and yet they have
managed to retain high standards.

It is a typical wine bar in style, with a blackboard menu,
stoneware pottery crockery, smoky atmosphere, a dark interior
and casual service. It is the sort of place to go for a snack and
wine rather than a main meal.

For vegetarians there is a choice of soup, or quiche and
salads. These change daily.

The sweets are a mixture of bought in and home-made.

Open: 12-2, 6-10.15 Monday-Saturday
Credit cards: none
60 seats

🍾 📃 🚭

Good Taste

44 Market Street, Llangollen, Clwyd, Wales, LL20 8PT
☎ 0978 861425
 £3

This vegetarian tea room, run by Mrs Roberts, is a real find. It is only small, but spotlessly clean, and serves only home-made food. Some of the recipes are on sale in the form of a little booklet.

The decor is charming with pale pink under-cloths and lace table-cloths. Outside they have cultivated a wonderful patio, set out with white garden furniture.

Although it is described as a tea room, Good Taste has plenty more than simply afternoon tea on offer. There are starters of mushroom pâté or egg mayonnaise. The main courses include vegetable cobbler, mushroom vol-au-vents with jacket potato, savoury pancake or quiche. For more of a snack, there are filled or open sandwiches, jacket potatoes, scones, buttered toast with a choice of breads.

Traditional-style sweets include apple or lemon meringue pie, pear belle helene and ice-cream.

Everything is very reasonably priced and packed lunches can be made to order.

The atmosphere is homely, the service excellent and you can choose to speak German, French, Welsh or English!

Open: 10-6 Monday-Saturday (weekends only in January,
     closed February)
Credit cards: none
20 seats plus patio

The Great Oak Café ✓

12 Great Oak Street, Llanidloes, Powys, Wales, SY18 6BU
☎ 05512 3211
🏠 £4

This café is run by a small co-operative of six people and has been established about five years. It's quite typical of the vegetarian style — earthy and arty — but the food is good, very cheap and wholesome, and the atmosphere is very friendly.

The menu is written on a blackboard and changes daily. Soup usually vegan, and salads with vegan and vegetarian dressings act as starters or lighter meals, then there are about five or six main courses, of which at least four will be vegan. There are substantial dishes such as lentil or nut roast, served with hot vegetables and gravy, which really sets you up for the day, or quiche, which goes well with the salad choice. There are also curries, pizza (also to take-away), vegeburgers and rolls, which are all home-made.

For puddings there are sweets, such as trifle or fruit salad, but also a good range of wholemeal cakes and biscuits — some plain, some iced. In this selection there will be some that are dairy- and egg-free. You can have these with a choice of soya or ordinary yoghurt.

Herbal teas and fruit juices are available and the tea and coffee sold here is bought from Traidcraft who use their profits to support Third World development.

It may all sound rather worthy, but there is an easy-going feel here that makes it a good place to go for a simple wholefood meal.

Open: 9.30-3 Monday, 9.30-5 Tuesday-Saturday
Credit cards: none
38 seats
🍴 🍷 ⊘ section

Herbs Cookshop

30 Mount Street, Bangor, Gwynned, Wales, LL57 1BG
☎ 0248 351249
 £2

Bangor is much in need of a wholefood vegetarian restaurant, but don't despair. You can either make your way to Jodies Wine Bar on the Menai Bridge (see next page), or go for a picnic-style meal by stocking up at this excellent take-away.

Herbs is in the tiny front room of a terraced house that, although only just behind the main shopping area, feels very much in the back streets. In fact, the person who gave me directions told me not to be put off by the unpromising surroundings!

Eighty per cent of Herbs' menu is vegetarian and they use free-range eggs. I tried a savoury pastry roll, filled with a mixture of cheese and soya. It looked considerably more appetizing than my description of it, was tasty cold and probably even better hot. I also had a sweet vegan carob and raisin bar. This meal totalled the princely sum of 75p!

The pizzas, quiches and cakes looked plain and wholesome.

The owners of Herbs are hoping to open a kiosk somewhere on the main street in 1989. I asked whether they had plans to open a restaurant and the answer, sadly, was 'Not yet'.

Open: 10-6 Monday-Saturday (closes 2pm Wednesday)
Credit cards: none
0 seats

♿ ⚕ ◯ �‖ 🚭

Jodies Wine Bar

Telford Road, Menai Bridge, Anglesey, Wales, LL59 5DT
☎ 0248 714864
♉ £7

The address is Menai Bridge and Jodies Wine Bar could scarcely be closer to it, as it is on the corner of the very first roundabout you come to as you leave the bridge on the Anglesey side. In fact, if you sit in the front rooms of this wine bar, you get an alarming close-up of the traffic whizzing by! Luckily there is room to sit at the back. When I visited, they had just completed a most delightful conservatory, overlooking the Menai Straits.

The tables are nicely spaced and the decor has a fresh, floral feel, in keeping with the style of the room. In the rest of the eating areas, the decor is darker and more intimate.

Jodies offers two menus. In the restaurant there are always two hot vegetarian main courses, which often have a wholefood emphasis. When I went, there was a curry with brown rice, or wholewheat spaghetti with vegetable sauce. You may also find lasagne or moussaka. In summer, there is a help-yourself salad table and usually some vegetarian quiches. The soup is generally vegetarian, too.

The puddings are on fairly traditional lines with liqueur ice-creams, sliced banana and meringue, and a chocolate mousse cake. A more interesting alternative was the blackcurrent purée, layered with yoghurt.

In the wine bar, you have more snack-style dishes, such as jacket potatoes, sandwiches, or spicy Mexican dip.

Whether you choose the restaurant or wine bar, the system is the same. You order at the counter and the food is brought to your table.

The atmosphere is lively and the staff friendly.

Open: 12-2, 7-10 Monday-Sunday restaurant, 11-2, 6-10
      Monday-Sunday wine bar
Credit cards: none
70 seats in restaurant, 50 seats in wine bar

Marton Rural Crafts Centre

The Old School, Marton, Welshpool, Powys, Wales, SY21 8JT
☎ 093872 341
🏠 £2

This is more a place for a decent morning coffee or afternoon tea rather than a full vegetarian meal, but it's worth going not just for the food — home-made cakes, scones, good sandwiches and first-class date and walnut cake — but also for the crafts displayed and in the process of being made. There are evening demonstrations too of weaving where food and wine is served, but for these you need to book.

The Centre is in a converted school. The desks have given way to natural wood tables, covered with gingham table-cloths. There's a spotless kitchen and the food is served on tasteful earthenware pottery with matching teapots.

Apart from cakes, scones, home-made lemon curd and jams, the main savouries are good sandwiches with salad garnish. Although you can't buy wine here as the café is not licensed, the staff do not mind you bringing your own if you want to.

The service was friendly and efficient.

Note, too, that this is one of the few places with a special loo for the disabled.

Open: 10-7 Monday-Saturday, 12-7 Sunday
Credit cards: none
14 seats

The No. 1 Wine and Food Bar

1 Old Road, Llandudno, Gwynnedd, Wales, LL30 2HA
☎ 0492 75424
🏠 £8

This pretty, intimate wine bar is housed in a little Victorian street not far from Llandudno's sweeping bay and promenade. The decor is in keeping with the character of the street — warm colours, dark, polished, wooden bar, pretty pictures and light fittings. It is rather like an oasis in a sea of hotels offering the standard prawn cocktail/black forest gâteau-type meal.

The menu at No 1. is set out on a blackboard, and don't be put off by the one outside, which does not list any vegetarian food. Inside is a separate little board especially for vegetarians. I had a good Greek salad as a starter, followed by a tasty pasta Sicilian. This was tagliatelle verdi with peppers, onions and Stilton in a cream sauce. Also on offer was a rich aubergine bake, both a Spanish and a cheese and tomato omelette and cheese and mushroom crêpes.

I think vegans might find it hard to find a filling meal here, as most of the 'Hot specials' contained either cheese or eggs. Probably, though, the management would be able to cope with advanced warning.

The service is efficient if a little off-hand.

Open: 12-2, 7-10 daily
Credit cards: none
40 seats
♿ 🍾 📙 🚭

The Old Forge

1 High Street, St David's, Haverfordwest, Wales, SA62 6SA
☎ 0437 720 488
🏠 £6

The Old Forge has been established some four years and you'll
find it in the High Street, close to the cathedral. It is a busy
place and the manager was eager to please, even though we
were vegetarian!

There were four choices, including a chilli con carne, which,
despite the title, was meatless, though you could be forgiven for
feeling nervous! There was also a vegeburger with chips,
aubergine and mushroom lasagne, and butter bean and
vegetable *gratin*.

The atmosphere is quite informal and the place, apart from
being an old forge 'mock up', has a wine-bar feel to it. It is
useful to know about for a casual night out.

Open: 10-10 daily in summer, 10.30-3, 6-10 daily in winter
40 seats

The Old Rectory

Maentwrog, Blaenau Ffestiniog, Gwynedd, Wales, LL41 4HN
☎ 076685 305
🛏 £5

Classical music quietly plays in the background of this sixteenth
century rectory, adding to the atmosphere of this comfortable
restaurant. It is clearly not always so peaceful as there is an area
set aside for dancing and some live entertainment is
programmed during the summer months.

The menu for vegetarians is quite extensive, though the use of
soya meat analogues may not appeal to everyone.

For starters there is soup — perhaps lentil, orange and
coriander, or haricot bean with tomato and tarragon — humus,
ravioli, or deep-fried, battered mushrooms. The main courses are
substantial and largely predictable — lasagne, Somerset pie, nut
roast, but all are served with at least four different vegetables.

To follow there is a really fresh fruit salad, or conventional
puds, such as apple pie.

The Old Rectory epitomizes a traditional style of eating. It is a
good destination for a semi-formal meal out as you can be sure
of smart attentive service and a professional approach.

Open: 12-2, 6.30-9 daily
50 seats

The Quarry Shop

13 Maengwyn Street, Machynlleth, Powys, Wales, SY20 9AZ
☎ 0654 2624
🏠 £3

This is an unpretentious, cheap, simple, wholemeal café and the
food matches the style: hearty bowls of soup, slices of pizza,
'Hot special' main courses, chalked up behind the cluttered
counter and slabs of cake. These are prepared using a wide
range of wholefoods. The main courses might be stir-fry
vegetables with gado gado sauce and rice, or a buckwheat
savoury.

We were too late for lunch, but tucked in to a delicious
apricot slice and chose from a bewildering range of teas and
coffee. While we ate, there was a lovely aroma of baking, which
turned out to be tomorrow's Dundee cake and a baked tofu
cheesecake. They use tofu in both sweet and savoury dishes and
in fact, overall, there's a conscious effort to cater for vegans,
with soya milk to drink and vegan margarine to spread on your
bread. They also sell filled rolls, all home-made and baked daily,
and, in the winter, there is usually a hot pudding.

The café is set amidst a wholefood shop, so, while you are
eating, you can look at the various homoeopathic remedies,
ecological washing powders and soon, which are very much in
keeping with the philosophy of the place.

The Quarry Shop is an offshoot of the Centre for Alternative
Technology, which is just outside Machynlleth, set in an old
slate quarry. It is well worth a visit and the entrance fee is only
£2.30. See all the different methods of saving and creating
energy with natural resources. I particularly liked the rather
surreal pink pedestal basin standing in solitary glory in an
outside yard. You turn the taps to find really hot water, heated
by the solar panels near by.

The areas set up as miniature organic herb/vegetable/
ornamental gardens are fascinating. The explanations are very
comprehensive and give you plenty of food for thought.

There is a café here, too — serving very similar food to the
Quarry Shop, though it is prepared by different chefs — and it
has a well-stocked bookshop, covering all aspects of alternative
energy and self-sufficiency.

Open: 9-3, 3.30-4.30 Monday-Wednesday, 9-2, 3.30-4.30
    Thursday, 9-3, 3.30-4.30 Friday and Saturday
Credit cards: none
30 seats

Sage

Unit 3, Wellfield Court, Roath, Cardiff, Wales, CF2 3NZ
☎ 0222 481223
🏠 £5

Sage is a wholefood vegetarian restaurant tucked away in
Wellfield Court, which is one of Cardiff's many shopping
centres. Unit 3 isn't the most attractive sounding address, but
the restaurant is very nicely decorated with apple white walls,
stripped pine benches and tables, wooden blinds and a little
awning outside where you can sit when it is warmer.

Downstairs is the open-plan kitchen and a few tables are
reserved for non-smokers, the main eating area being upstairs.

Everything is home-made and there are a variety of soups plus
a choice of hot main courses. The main courses are usually
contrasting casseroles, such as chilli or hot pot, and layered
bakes, like lasagne or moussaka. One of these is usually suitable
for vegans too. There is also either a flan or a pizza and a
choice of five salads, which vary tremendously depending on
what is in season.

Puddings include cheesecake, crumbles and so on, and, again,
these very according to what fruit is available. There are also
plenty of wholesome cakes, some of which are sugar-free. They
try to use organic produce whenever possible.

Food is good value here and Sage is a friendly place to get a
decent day-time meal.

Open: 9-5 Monday-Saturday (lunch from 11.45)
Credit cards: none
50 seats
 section

Small Planet

3 Agincourt Street, Monmouth, Gwent, Wales, NP5 3DZ
☎ 0600 2995
🏠 £3

Monmouth is a very attractive town, and the drive to it from
Chepstow, up the Wye valley, past the glorious Tintern Abbey
is delightful. I arrived here just as everything was closing at
5pm, and was more than amazed to find this tiny little eating
place behind a clean, smart-looking wholefood shop in the
central market square.

Two young girls at the counter looked a little dismayed to
have such a late customer, but were nevertheless friendly and
apologized for the lack of choice. I settled for take-away quiches.
Both were absolutely delicious, with good, thick fillings and
nutty pastry. One had a celery and walnut filling and the other
onion.

The café has been established about two years and is
deservedly becoming very popular. There is an emphasis on
using top-quality wholefoods, organic wherever possible. They
also endeavour to cater for special diets, including vegan and
low-sugar items on the menu.

Basic soup starts at 50p, with more elaborate concoctions,
such as broad bean and hazelnut perhaps setting you back a
princely 75p! There are hot main courses — quiches, as I've
mentioned, pasties and several salads.

There were good home-made cakes and 16 different teas.

The full menu is served all day, and I had the feeling that if
you arrived at a more appropriate time than I did for a meal,
you would be well looked after.

Open: 9-5 Monday-Saturday
Credit cards: none
25 seats

Waverley Restaurant ✓

23 Lammas Street, Carmarthen, Wales, SA31 3AL
☎ 0267 236521
🏠 £4

We arrived rather late in the day at the Waverley Restaurant and
the cupboard was just about bare! However, we got some
supplies from the shop at the front of the building, which was
very well stocked, and brought them back into the restaurant to
make a meal. It seemed common practice.

The place is evidently popular although I found it a little
barrack-like, and the counter was not very appealing.

The menu has all the standard vegetarian wholefood offerings,
such as quiches, a range of salads, jacket potatoes, hot
savouries, such as lasagne, or nut burgers. On quieter days and
out of season, there is a choice of three or four main courses,
but when times are busier they have as many as six. They tend
to make one lot, in fairly large quantities, I should imagine, and,
when that runs out, that is it! Fortunately there was a little nut
roast left, which was good, moist and had a good texture.

The cakes we had from the shop were good. Usually available
are fruit salad, pie such as apple, and cheesecake.

There was a large range of herbal teas, which, unlike the
ordinary tea which comes in pots, is just served in a cup with
one tea bag floating round. Still they were willing to give me a
pot of hot water as well so I had more than enough to drink,
and at my preferred strength.

The Waverley Restaurant is a useful place for a wholefood bite
to eat if you're in the vicinity of Carmarthen or *en route* to West
Wales.

Open: 9-4.30 Monday-Wednesday, 9-2 Thursday, 9-4.30 Friday
and Saturday
Credit cards: none
50 seats

The Whole Thing

5 Field Street, Llangefni, Isle of Anglesey, Gwynedd, Wales,
LL77 7EH
☎ 0248 724832
🏠 £4

The Whole Thing is an excellent, small, wholefood shop and a
first floor café. The shop is jam-packed with every shelf and
possible space loaded with packages, bags and bottles. A host
of colours and aromas greet the senses as you walk in. The café
above, by comparison, seems rather plain. It is a light, airy
room with a few modern, wood tables and the walls haphazardly
adorned with the odd picture. Strangely, there was little food to
see on the serving counter, even though we were there at the
beginning of the lunch-time period: a couple of hot dishes were
in a warming cupboard, a plate of cakes was tucked away
underneath the counter and there were a few boxes of drinks
behind the counter, but no sign of salads. I didn't feel they were
doing much to tempt the appetite, which was a shame as what
we had was very good.
  I had a tasty pizza with a crunchy seed topping and a crisp
side-salad. The soup was rather dull — cream of tomato — but
served with good bread. Main dishes on offer vary but include
the usual pastas, curries, and *croustade*. These were all served
with salads. There is usually a savoury flan, using seasonal
vegetables, too.
  The range of home-made cakes was particularly good.
  All the cheese used is vegetarian, the eggs are free-range and
the flour is wholemeal. They will also let you bring and drink
your own wine as they have no licence to sell alcohol.
  I liked this place. The service was friendly, the room pleasant,
but I just felt they could do so much more to attract people in
to eat what is evidently simple, wholesome food.

Open: 9-5.30 Monday-Friday
Credit cards: none
32 seats

Geographical index

278

Restaurant index

Your Comments

Please send this page, or a photocopy, (you don't need stamps) to:

Sarah Brown's Best of Vegetarian Britain
Thorsons Publishers Limited,
FREEPOST,
Wellingborough,
Northamptonshire NN8 2BR

Name of restaurant:
Address:

Phone no:
Date of last visit:
Completely vegetarian, or do they serve meat as well?

What was the atmosphere like?

Were the staff friendly and helpful?

What dishes are especially worth mentioning?

What did your meal cost?
Any other comments?

Your name and address: